Contents

PSYCHOSOCIAL ADJUSTMENT TO DISABILITY

PSYCHOSOCIAL ADJUSTMENT TO DISABILITY

by
Richard Roessler, Ph.D.
Associate Professor
Brian Bolton, Ph.D.
Associate Professor

With the Assistance of
Daniel Cook, Greta Mack, Bob Means, and **Tim Milligan**
Arkansas Rehabilitation Research and Training Center,
University of Arkansas, Fayetteville

UNIVERSITY PARK PRESS
Baltimore

UNIVERSITY PARK PRESS
International Publishers in Science and Medicine
233 East Redwood Street
Baltimore, Maryland 21202

Typeset by Action Comp. Co., Inc.
Manufactured in the United States of America by The Maple Press Company

Library of Congress Cataloging in Publication Data

Roessler, Richard, 1944-
    Psychosocial adjustment to disability.

    Includes bibliographical references and index.
    1. Handicapped—Psychology.   2. Handicapped.
I. Bolton, Brian, 1939–   joint author.   II. Title.
HV3000.R63   362.4   78-5646
ISBN 0-8391-1244-0

Preface

Because of the importance of clients' psychosocial adjustment in successful rehabilitation programming, the Arkansas Rehabilitation Research and Training Center has focused a major research and development effort on psychosocial adjustment strategies during the past six years. *Psychosocial Adjustment to Disability* summarizes the results of empirical research and describes the training packages that have emanated from this sustained effort.

The volume is organized around three main themes: the effects of disablement on personal adjustment, the process of adjusting to disability, and techniques and strategies for enhancing psychosocial adjustment to disability. Hence, this is a unique book in the "psychological aspects of disability" literature in that the central concern is adjustment, with special emphasis on techniques for facilitating optimal adjustment to disability.

Psychosocial Adjustment to Disability was designed to serve as a textbook for several courses in rehabilitation counseling training programs and other health-related and special education training programs, and as a resource manual for practitioners and inservice training supervisors in the helping professions. In particular, a major consideration in preparing *Psychosocial Adjustment* was to minimize overlap with the dozen or so "psychological aspects" books that are currently available; e.g., Albrecht (1976), Barker, et al. (1953), Cobb (1973), Garrett and Levine (1962), McDaniel (1976), Marinelli and Dell Orto (1977), Neff (1971), Safilios-Rothschild (1970), Shontz (1975), Stubbins (1977), Sussman (1965), and Wright (1960). Thus, *Psychosocial Adjustment* can be used as the primary text for various educational and training purposes, or in conjunction with one of the more traditional texts listed above.

Furthermore, *Psychosocial Adjustment* is oriented to all types of disablement—physical, psychiatric, intellectual, and social. However, special emphasis is given to the severely disabled, with a separate chapter on spinal cord injury. Three chapters provide descriptions of comprehensive training packages—Personal Achievement Skills, Physical Fitness Training, and Behavior Analysis Training—and summarize the research that supports their usefulness in rehabilitation programming. Although the orientation of the volume is practical, as opposed to theoretical, we have reviewed and summarized relevant research whenever appropriate. Each chapter contains one or more sections that present the results of research studies reported in the literature and/or describe major research projects conducted under the auspices of the Arkansas Rehabilitation Research and Training Center. Thus, *Psychosocial Adjustment* is both research-based and practitioner-oriented.

Copies of the training packages and research reports, which are listed in the References, can be obtained from the Publications Office, Arkansas Rehabilitation Research and Training Center, Hot Springs Rehabilitation Center, Hot Springs, Arkansas 71901, or The Clearinghouse of Rehabilitation Materials, Oklahoma State University, Stillwater, Oklahoma 74074. Because

viii Preface

the Research and Training Center is a nonprofit organization, all publications are available free or for a small printing and handling charge.

Four of our colleagues are listed on the title page as collaborators in the authorship of *Psychosocial Adjustment to Disability*. We wish to acknowledge their specific contributions: Dan Cook is co-investigator on the Spinal Cord Injury Project (chapter 4), Greta Mack was co-investigator on the Regional Integrated Services Project (chapter 9), Bob Means co-authored the Personal Achievement Skills and Behavior Analysis Training packages (chapters 6 and 8), and Tim Milligan authored the Physical Fitness Training package (chapter 7). However, we assume full responsibility for the presentations in this book.

Finally, we wish to acknowledge the support of Rehabilitation Services Administration Grant 16-P-56812, RT-13 to the Arkansas Rehabilitation Research and Training Center, and to emphasize that the publication of *Psychosocial Adjustment to Disability* is a nonprofit project on the part of the authors. We also want to express our appreciation to Paul Brookes, Executive Editor of University Park Press, and his staff. Special thanks are given to Steve Boone and Jerry Henderson for preparing the indexes, and to David Sigman for the cover design.

Chapter 1

Psychosocial Adjustment in Rehabilitation

Certain fundamental psychological concepts and practical issues are essential to an understanding of the role of personal adjustment training in rehabilitation services. These basic concepts and issues are discussed in this chapter. Three parties are involved directly or indirectly in the rehabilitation process—the client, the rehabilitation professional, and the society that endorses and supports this complex, humanitarian endeavor. Throughout the book, we emphasize the psychological effects of disablement on the client and describe the process of adjustment to disability. The second party in the rehabilitation process, the rehabilitation practitioner, views the process primarily as a problem of how to enhance clients' motivation in order to increase their participation and ensure their ultimate success. Society's collective impact on disabled individuals is transmitted in the form of highly variable and often ambivalent attitudes toward disability and disabled persons.

Because this book was designed to serve as a manual for rehabilitation practitioners, it is appropriate to begin by addressing their major concern—client motivation. The most often cited reason for client failure in rehabilitation is "lack of motivation." When 280 rehabilitation counselors in a five-state area responded to the question "What problems do you see in counseling and vocational planning as stemming from characteristics of the client himself?" almost one-half (43%) gave lack of motivation as their first choice (Thoreson et al., 1968, p. 19). An analysis of the verbatim responses by the counselors revealed six specific areas of perceived difficulty:

1. The client feels hopeless, depressed, disheartened, etc., because of his disability and/or other limitations

2. The client ascribes an authoritarian role to counselor and assumes a passive one for himself
3. The client is receiving some form of financial aid which he feels rehabilitation will disrupt
4. Unrealistic vocational goals are maintained by the client
5. Undesirable personal characteristics, e.g., aggressiveness, hostility, immaturity, etc., are exhibited by the client
6. Low labor market demand exists for client services

It is apparent from these six patterns that "lack of client motivation" includes internal referents (e.g., hopelessness, depression, passivity, immaturity, etc.) as well as situational or environmental problems (e.g., the counselor's role, secondary gains from the disability, "tight" labor market, including unfavorable attitudes toward the disabled, etc.). In other words, the concept of motivation in rehabilitation encompasses all aspects of behavior—a conclusion reached from extensive literature reviews by Barry and Malinovsky (1965) and Lane and Barry (1970). These authors also concluded that "... there is a great deal more which needs to be known about the dynamics of rehabilitation" (Barry and Malinovsky, 1965, p. 59), and "Instead of treating motivation as some vaguely defined internal entity it will certainly be more useful to deal with a behavior in terms of the variables of which it is a function" (Lane and Barry, 1970, p. 23).

Several conclusions can be drawn from the above survey results and discussion: 1) the concept of motivation is an important explanatory variable in rehabilitation counseling, at least as viewed by the practitioner, 2) lack of motivation is truly a multidimensional construct, encompassing all types of psychosocial problems—personal, social, vocational, and societal, and 3) the only feasible approach to dealing with the "unmotivated client" is one that focuses on the specific behavioral deficits that can be identified. Finally, we believe that the personal adjustment training programs that are outlined in subsequent chapters of this book provide the most effective "motivational techniques" that are currently available for use by rehabilitation practitioners in working with their clients.

PERSONAL ADJUSTMENT TRAINING

From at least two different points of view, adjustment services in rehabilitation are important activities provided for clients. The first point of view sees psychosocial adjustment as a goal of parallel importance to the goals of vocational training and placement. The second point of view emphasizes that psychosocial adjustment is a necessary prerequisite for achieving employment and making a satisfactory vocational adjustment. Regardless of the point of view adopted, a valid argument can be advanced for offering personal adjustment training concurrently with vocational training. Clarifying whether clients' psychosocial adjustment is a process that occurs independently of vocational success, or is a necessary prerequisite to it, is an important question for rehabilitation research, and is reviewed later in this chapter. However, for the rehabilitation practitioner, ample evidence exists to support personal adjustment training as a valuable service in rehabilitation; several supportive studies are reviewed in subsequent chapters.

Personal adjustment training is an area in which clients learn the appropriate skills and/or behaviors necessary to become adequately functioning persons and productive community members. In other words, such services contribute considerably to rehabilitation's overall goal of helping the client learn "to live as a disabled individual within one's own environment" (Trieschmann, 1974, p. 556). But, adjustment training, because it deals with the complexities of human behavior, is one of the less well defined and understood aspects of rehabilitation (Baker and Sawyer, 1971). Little agreement exists regarding the meaning of the concept of adjustment and of the services to be rendered in its behalf. The problem is further complicated by adding the concept of disability and speaking of "adjustment to disability."

ISSUES IN DEFINING ADJUSTMENT

Though it is difficult to get complete agreement about the meaning of adjustment, some generalized definitions draw upon the biological concept of adaptation. For example, Lazarus (1969) defined adjustment to include "man's efforts, successful and unsuccessful, to deal with life in the face of environmental demands, internal pressures, and human potentials" (p. x). However, he indicated that adjustment can be looked at from a number of viewpoints, such as achievement versus process. Sechrest and Wallace (1967) added several other issues: frame of reference, measurability, cultural point of view, homogeneity/heterogeneity, and continuous or discontinuous. The first two issues—achievement versus process, and frame of reference—have special relevance to the subject of adjustment to disability and, thus, are reviewed in some depth in this section.

Adjustment—Achievement or Process

One approach to adjustment defines it as a state or goal that can be accomplished well or badly (Lazarus, 1969). There are several difficulties with the state or goal notion of adjustment. For example, the concept of adjustment is not defined, nor are the steps for becoming adjusted clarified. Because people see adjustment as a trouble-free state, they come to over-value the concept. Also, individuals develop unrealistically high expectations about what they should be able to accomplish in their lives. Unfortunately, the goal concept presumes that all problems are solvable and does not prepare one to deal with the senseless aspects of life, such as disability, disease, and natural disaster (Sechrest and Wallace, 1967).

A process definition of adjustment, on the other hand, does not imply that life will ever be trouble-free. Instead, it focuses on how people meet stress and on what events influence their efforts to adapt to it. The process concept implies that individuals must deal with a succession of situations, each with its own peculiar demands. Existence is a process of continually adjusting to the situations and their inherent problems, all of which require a response from the individual. Adjustment is defined in terms of the adequacy of the way in which the person responds to life situations. The adjusted person is generally effective in resolving life's problems, while the maladjusted person is overwhelmed by life's problems.

Frame of Reference

Two frames of reference, or perspectives, exist for judging the degree of a person's adjustment or maladjustment. The first perspective is that of the individual, and is ascertained via self-report. However, the problem of self-report, or asking the person if he/she is adjusted, leads to the following paradoxical situation, supported by research. There is some indication that the less self-knowledge people have, and the less inclined they are to examine themselves, the more likely they are to report high levels of self-satisfaction and self-adjustment (Sechrest and Wallace, 1967). Of course, in many cases, the judgment of adjustment or maladjustment is made by an external agent; e.g., a psychologist, a psychiatrist, a rehabilitation counselor, or in some situations, a family member. The judgments by external agents, who represent the second perspective or frame of reference, are usually professionally rendered and absolutely necessary. It follows, then, that a question of great importance in the assessment of clients' adjustment is the extent of convergence between the two perspectives.

A recent article by Bolton (1978a) discusses the problem of differential viewpoints in the initial assessment of client rehabilitation needs or level of adjustment, and summarizes the results of a statistical study of client and counselor judgments. In this investigation, a sample of clients who had been accepted for rehabilitation services completed the Human Service Scale and were evaluated by their counselors using the Client Outcome Measure. Thus, the psychosocial adjustment of the clients was evaluated from two perspectives—client (self) and counselor (external agent)—using standard multiscale instruments that purport to measure several common dimensions, e.g., physical condition, vocational/economic status, and family relationships. Although the statistical analyses suggested a trend toward convergence, the modest size of the correlations (the highest was 0.42) indicates that clients and counselors are seldom in close agreement in their independent judgments.

When compared to the results of research in the domain of psychopathology, this result is seen to fall well within the range of previously obtained relationships. Nine studies of interperspective convergence conducted in psychiatric settings produced correlations that ranged from nonsignificant to high (Bolton, 1977b). However, a statistical study reported in the article by Bolton (1977b), using a sample of rehabilitation clients with emotional disabilities, concluded that "within the limits of unreliability, psychologist and client perspectives converge to the same global assessment of extent of psychopathology" (p. 538). About all that can be concluded regarding the issue of frame of reference in defining and measuring clients' adjustment is that the extent of agreement depends upon a number of factors, e.g., type of instrument, nature of the psychosocial domain, purpose of the assessment, etc.

CONCEPTS OF ADJUSTMENT

The various dimensions of adjustment can be seen in most popular and scientific definitions of the term. In this section, several thumbnail sketches of adjustment models have been adapted from Sechrest and Wallace (1967) to illustrate the wide range of approaches to the conceptualization of adjustment.

Survival Model

The survival model of adjustment emphasizes the idea that behaviors are adjustive or appropriate if they keep the person alive, healthy, and able to reproduce the species. However, survival is an all or none, or discontinuous, concept, in that one is either alive or dead. Furthermore, it seems somewhat irrelevant in a highly technical, affluent culture, but not altogether—there are many individuals for whom the survival issue is of utmost importance. Because there are no value standards beyond survival, the model can be used to justify such reprehensible behavior as that exhibited by Hitler in the name of the survival of the German state.

Medical Model

Another model of adjustment, the medical model, has been extremely important in the development of psychology. It assumes that there is a cause for maladjustment that underlies observable behavioral symptoms. It is crucial, according to the model, that one not treat the symptoms but the underlying cause for the maladjustment. Little is said about what adjustment is other than that it reflects the absence of some underlying condition that causes maladjustment.

There are many problems with the medical model that can be identified. It overemphasizes internal states or controlling mechanisms at the expense of environmental forces and constraints. For the most part, it is difficult to identify and reliably measure pathology. The medical model is dichotomous in two senses: it focuses on healthy or unhealthy states, and it assumes that some kind of fixed goal of adjustment is achieved upon treatment of the underlying cause.

Positive Striving Model

A somewhat more comprehensive and differentiated model of adjustment has been developed that emphasizes a dimensional viewpoint. Adjustment is seen as including: 1) positive self-regard and veridical self-awareness, 2) a tendency to fulfill unique potential or to self-actualize, 3) an integration or organization of personality, 4) an accurate perception of reality, 5) a relative freedom from need distortion of perceptions, 6) an autonomy or capacity for independent behavior, 7) environmental mastery manifested in adequacy in love, work, and play in interpersonal relationships and in situational contexts, and 8) efficiency in problem solving.

The positive striving model, according to Sechrest and Wallace, has many desirable features. For example, it is process oriented, and it covers a wide range of behavior. The model is continuous in stressing degrees of adjustment in each of the various areas. However, each aspect of the positive striving concept reflects a value judgment as to what is beneficial for individuals. Furthermore, there are obvious measurement problems with such concepts as self-actualization, self-esteem, etc.

Other Models of Adjustment

The positive striving and medical models in many ways represent major themes in psychology. The medical model has been the basis for psychoanalytic theory and therapy, whereas the positive striving model parallels the humanistic approach to psychology. However, psychology is a diverse field, and there are many other models of adjustment that exist (Sechrest and Wallace, 1967). For example, the tension reduction model defines adjustment as the individual's ability to reduce need tension or drive. People are poorly adjusted to the extent that they are unable to meet their needs and to the extent that they come into conflict with others who are trying to meet personal needs.

Another interesting model of adjustment having potential for psychology is the engineering model, which focuses on optimal functioning. The engineering model stresses study of individual capabilities and situational demands before deciding whether or not the person is performing as he or she should. The key question is whether or not demonstrated efficiency is in a direct one-to-one ratio with potential efficiency. If so, the person is deemed adjusted; if not, maladjusted.

Other adjustment models exist, but do not have the same scientific validity or potential as the ones previously mentioned. For example, it is possible to view adjustment as a social conformity phenomenon, in which the compatibility of individual and social goals is stressed. The theme is "what is good for society is good for the individual." A counter to the social conformity model is the self-satisfaction model, which turns the previous statement around to simply "what is good for the individual is good for society." Another model is the legal/ethical notion of adjustment, in which maladjustment is defined simply as those things not permitted by law. The statistical model of adjustment holds that behaviors falling outside of the statistically normal range are viewed as maladjusted. There are obviously many problems with these models, so it suffices to say that they do not provide a sound basis for the development of an adjustment model for rehabilitation.

PSYCHOSOCIAL ADJUSTMENT AND VOCATIONAL ADJUSTMENT

The relationship between psychosocial adjustment and vocational adjustment is not clear at this time. Although there is considerable empirical evidence indicating that they are correlated, the causal nature of the relationship has not been established. Differences in research design and the overall complexity of the issue have prevented researchers from clarifying the direction of influence in the relationship between these two major classes of variables. This section outlines the issue and reviews relevant research results.

First, it should be emphasized that, until very recently, the only justification for including personal adjustment training in rehabilitation services was the argument that enhanced psychosocial adjustment increased the probability of successful job placement and long-term vocational adjustment. Ironically, the implicit assumption underlying the focus on employment as the only criterion of rehabilitation success was that, because of its central importance in American values, work would lead to improvements in clients' subsequent personal and social adjustment. It is apparent, then, that some kind of interfacilitative relationship between psychosocial adjustment and vocational adjustment has always been part of the vocational rehabilitation philosophy.

Research Review

Studies that are relevant to the issue fall into two distinct categories: 1) experimental investigations in which a sample of clients receives some type of personal adjustment training and is then assessed in terms of improvement on various work-related variables, and 2) correlational studies in which two or more psychosocial and vocational variables are measured and intercorrelated for a sample of clients. Because the experimental studies are reviewed in conjunction with the presentation of personal adjustment programs in later chapters, only the correlational investigations are summarized here.

Two studies have examined the relationship between self-esteem and vocational outcome. MacGuffie et al. (1969) studied a sample of applicants for state rehabilitation services and found that clients with higher self-concepts were more likely to have been closed in employment. In a multivariable investigation using a sample of physically disabled clients, Barry, Dunteman, and Webb (1968) isolated a relationship between favorable attitudes toward self and return to work.

Three other predictive studies provide relevant evidence. The Minnesota Multiphasic Personality Inventory (MMPI) Hypochondriasis scale correlated significantly with employment status four months after the occurrence of heart attacks for a sample of cardiac patients (Gressett, 1969). Ayer, Thoreson, and Butler (1966) correlated 14 MMPI scales with employment outcome for a sample of state rehabilitation clients: none of the correlations exceeded 0.10. Lastly, Schwartz, Dennerll, and Lin (1968) found several relationships between employment and various scales of the Edwards Personal Preference Schedule (EPPS) and the California Personality Inventory (CPI) for a sample of clients with epilepsy. The highest correlation was with the CPI self-acceptance scale, a result that is consistent with the findings of the first two studies reviewed above.

Generally, these research results suggest that clients who report better psychosocial adjustment have a greater probability of becoming vocationally successful after appropriate rehabilitation services are provided. However, these predictive investigations do *not* address another aspect of the question—that of the relationship between changes or improvements in psychosocial and vocational adjustment during the rehabilitation process.

One of the authors has analyzed the correlations among change scores on psychosocial and vocational variables for two samples of state rehabilitation clients (Bolton, 1974a; 1978c). In the first study, a factor analysis of 12 psychosocial change scores derived from the pre/post administrations of two standard instruments and from three vocational change scores based on work status and salary produced three factors. The factor identified as improved vocational functioning was uncorrelated with the two psychosocial adjustment factors. It was tentatively concluded that psychosocial adjustment and vocational success are independent dimensions of client change during the rehabilitation process. The second study was designed to remedy weaknesses in the initial investigation. While the results were partially supportive of the conclusion of the first study, viz., psychosocial and vocational change dimensions were distinguishable, one additional relationship emerged. Clients' self-reported changes in emotional security were consistently correlated with their counselors' evaluations of their improvements in all areas of functioning, including vocational adjustment.

As is so often the case with social science research, straightforward, unequivocal conclusions are not immediately apparent in this review. Although there are no instances of directly contradictory findings, it is difficult to synthesize the results of predictive studies and change-score analyses, univariate and dimensional approaches, and correlational and experimental investigations. Nevertheless, we

believe that the following general conclusion is warranted: psychosocial adjustment and vocational improvement tend to occur concurrently, with a bidirectional or mutual influence process accounting
for the covariation. In other words, psychosocial adjustment en-
hances vocational success and vice versa.

ATTITUDES TOWARD DISABILITY

The negative attitudes that the majority of nondisabled persons have
toward disability constitute a virtually insurmountable barrier to fair
treatment and equality of opportunity for handicapped persons. The
pervasiveness of unfavorable attitudes toward disabled persons is
well summarized by Gellman (1959):

> Prejudice toward handicapped persons with their open or hidden re-
> jection by the nonhandicapped occurs at all socio-economic levels and
> in all regions of our country. It is evident in the social, educational,
> and vocational discriminations which hamper disabled persons. It is
> obvious in the institutional gates which separate the severely disabled
> from the community of the nondisabled. It is apparent in the dif-
> ficulties which the handicapped face in securing employment. It is
> clearly manifest in the self-depreciation of the disabled (p. 20).

Regardless of the type of disabling condition, whether physical,
intellectual, emotional, or social, or whether functional or cosmetic,
the afflicted person is at a substantial disadvantage and faces many
unnecessary difficulties, if not overwhelming odds, in striving to
adjust in a society that values good health, athletic prowess, and
personal appearance. In this section, some basic information about
the nature of attitudes toward disabled persons is presented, and
some suggestions for addressing the problems of prejudice and discrimination are outlined. A preliminary statement regarding terminology is appropriate here: negative or prejudicial attitudes act to
stigmatize or devalue disabled persons, and the result is usually
discriminatory behavior directed at the disabled population.

Some Conclusions

An enormous number of research investigations have examined
various aspects of the subject of attitudes toward disability. The conclusions listed below were extracted from the classic review by Barker et al. (1953) and a recent summary by Siller (1976). Despite
the fact that the two publications are separated by almost a quarter
of a century, their conclusions are similar.

1. Attitudes toward disabled persons, while highly varied, are frequently negative. Public, verbalized attitudes are on the average mildly favorable. However, indirect evidence suggests that deeper unverbalized attitudes are more frequently hostile.
2. Society's rejecting attitudes toward the disabled result in greatly restricted vocational and social opportunities.
3. The attitudes of disabled persons toward their own disabilities have been inadequately studied. Furthermore, the available evidence indicates that the subject is complex, e.g., Weinberg-Asher (1976) found that disabled persons perceive themselves in much the same way that able-bodied persons perceive themselves; but Schroedel and Schiff (1972) concluded that deaf persons manifest more negative attitudes toward deafness than do hearing persons.
4. Attitudes toward the disabled are multidimensional in structure, i.e., there are from 10 to 12 relatively independent attitudinal components that account for unfavorable reactions to disabled persons.
5. Attempts to modify negative attitudes toward the disabled have generally been unsuccessful.
6. The evidence is rather clear that the attitudes of parents toward their disabled children tend to be extreme more often than the attitudes of parents toward their normal children.

Several of these conclusions deserve emphasis. First, attitudes toward disabled persons are typically unfavorable, despite what most people say when asked. Second, negative attitudes toward the disabled result in real barriers and restricted opportunities; again, prejudice produces discrimination against disabled persons. Third, the unfavorable attitudes held by nondisabled persons may influence disabled persons' views of their worth, although Weinberg-Asher (1976) interpreted her findings to "seriously question the theoretical position that the disabled introject the majority's view of them as different" (p. 19). Fourth, disabled persons often live with unfavorable attitudes from a very early age because even their parents may have difficulty treating them normally.

Origins of Attitudes Toward Disability

Whether prejudicial attitudes toward the disabled reflect some kind of natural aversion to deviations in physique or behavior, or can be explained by a developmental social learning theory, there can be no question about the depth of the roots of negative attitudes toward disability. One indication of the tenacity of these attitudes is the inability of psychologists to change them (see the fifth conclusion stated above). Gellman (1959) outlined four sources or roots of prejudice against the handicapped:

1. Social customs and norms that emphasize youth, wholeness, and bodily perfection
2. Child-rearing practices that stress normalcy and health
3. The recrudescence of neurotic childhood fears in frustrating or anxiety-provoking situations
4. Prejudice by invitation—discrimination-provoking behavior by the disabled

We believe that the first three of Gellman's sources can be organized in a three-step sequence that helps to explain prejudice and discrimination against disabled persons: 1) nondisabled persons are fearful of disablement, disfigurement, loss of sensory capacity, loss of self-control, etc.; 2) therefore, contact with afflicted persons causes intense discomfort and arouses anxiety; and 3) hence, disabled persons are avoided and efforts are made to segregate them and isolate them.

Combating Prejudice and Discrimination

The fourth source of prejudice noted by Gellman is potentially under the control of disabled persons. The implication is that they can learn to inhibit discrimination-provoking behaviors. Siller (1976) believes that disabled persons have a responsibility to acquire the social skills necessary to improve their interpersonal interactions with nondisabled persons. He thus recommends that "social coping skills should be part of any rehabilitation program" (Siller, 1976, p. 75). In addition to behavioral skills training, English (1971, p. 21) suggests that disabled persons should be educated about "a basic fact of life" for them—the existence and prevalence of stigmatizing attitudes toward them.

It should be obvious, then, that personal adjustment training for rehabilitation clients has even greater potential and wider ramifications than have been suggested heretofore. We believe that the strategies outlined in this volume can do much to give disabled clients more control over their lives, both through increased personal competence and enhanced interpersonal skills, as well as knowledge of their circumstances.

English (1971) has outlined several other strategies that may be useful in dealing with unfavorable public attitudes:

1. Increase the amount of meaningful contact between the disabled and the nondisabled
2. Influence the mass media to present more realistic views of disability and disabled persons
3. Include the client's family and significant others in the rehabilitation program
4. Encourage elected officials to review legislation that unnecessarily restricts the lives of the disabled
5. Promote and participate in citizen advocacy programs

UNDERSTANDING THE EFFECTS OF DISABILITY

Generally, disability, whether adventitious or congenital, is viewed as an acute physical and psychosocial shock. It is a discontinuous trauma for the individual, affecting biological, social, and vocational functioning. The effectiveness of one's body as a physical tool is diminished, and a loss of capacity for sensation, movement, or cerebration makes even the simplest tasks major obstacles (Barker et al., 1953).

Changes in one's physique and behaviors become stimuli new to self and to others. Body image and self-perceptions, often accompanied by negative feedback from others, lead to negative personal appraisals that can result in decreases in self-esteem. In addition, the phenomenal experience of loss is overwhelming and obviously experienced as a deprivation of extreme significance. The loss seemingly has no rhyme or reason, and leads one to ask, "Why me?"

Talking abstractly about the concept of disability is important on an analytic or scientific level; but, it is also important that the observer be empathic regarding the extreme significance of disability to an individual's life. As mentioned, from an abstract or analytic point of view, disability is a discontinuous experience that seriously disrupts person/environment fit. A conflict at this most basic level has great psychological significance, and will be appraised as such by many individuals. At the same time, it is important to remember that reaction to disability is a highly individualized matter that is a function of both the person and the environment.

Restorative Process

It seems fair to say that all individuals react to disability as an issue of grave importance and that there is a typical pattern of reaction to that disability. To some extent, observers agree that there is a common restorative process that occurs, including the following stages:

1. Denial—defending against the trauma by denying its existence
2. Mourning—grieving for the loss
3. Depression—characterized by questions such as "Why me?" and realizations such as "I will never be the same"
4. Anger—hostility directed at one's world for its injustices and toward others for their inability to understand
5. Positive coping—a review of the major tasks that remain to be completed

   After a comprehensive review of studies on human reaction to stress, Falek and Britton (1974) concluded that there is a predictable sequence of responses that are designed to enable the person to reestablish a "psychological steady state." They isolated the following sequence:

1. Denial—In order to maintain integrity of the personality, the individual simply denies the existence of a traumatic event. Common behavioral forms of denial include: a) being stunned or dazed, b) refusing to accept information, c) insisting there has been a mistake, d) not understanding what has been said.
2. Anxiety and Fear—Upon recognizing the traumatic event, the person experiences fear and anxiety regarding its effects. The anxiety may take the form of: a) generalized nervousness, b) overactivity, c) irritability, d) headaches, e) fatigue, f) insomnia, g) loss of appetite, and h) somatic complaints. To relieve the anxiety, the individual seeks information allowing a return to the previous state. Simon (1971) noted that these concerns include fears of loss of security, one's fantasied future, and love of spouse, family, and friends (p. 409).
3. Anger and Hostility—Without an emotional acceptance of the trauma, the individual finds that new information does not lead to effective ways to restore the previous state. Failure in efforts to reach the previous state leads, in some cases, to bitterness and hostility; in other cases, to guilt, a form of internalized anger.
4. Depression—Faced with failure, the individual loses hope of returning to the previous state and begins to be depressed. Personal manifestations include being withdrawn, showing lack of interest, or being sad.
5. Equilibrium—Depression precedes an emotional acceptance

that reflects a person's realization that he or she cannot function in the state of depression. To adjust to the situation, the individual tries new behaviors based on both an intellectual and emotional understanding. Of course, temporary frustrations may cause the person to go through the whole sequence again before establishing a new equilibrium.

Signs of Succumbing

There are, however, some key factors that can facilitate or impede the restorative process. Certainly, the individual's appraisal of the gravity of the disability's long term effect is important. Also, the experience of devaluing self and being devaluated by others can impede the adjustment. The effects of discrepant social expectations have a negative impact on disabled individuals, in that expectations of others stress that they act disabled. The individual must cope with the phenomenon of psychological spread, in which people perceive disabled individuals as limited in all aspects. Finally, the individual must cope with the requirement of mourning; that is, the disabled person is expected to mourn for the loss—in a sense, to repent for past errors (Wright, 1960).

Attempts are made to deal with negative social input and personal appraisals that in the short run seem to block devaluation and maintain self-esteem. But, according to Wright (1960), these are signs of succumbing, not coping:

1. "As if" behaviors—The individual attempts to conceal the disability; i.e., to act as if it does not exist.
2. Idolizing normal standards—The individual carries old value patterns into the new situation. Previous aspirations are not viewed in terms of the context of new limitations. Idolizing normal standards, unfortunately, builds in failure.
3. Eclipse of behavioral possibilities—The process of "as if" behaviors and idolizing normal standards does not allow disabled persons to learn what they can do and to learn new skills in order to be more effective.
4. Compensation—Disabled individuals try to make up for their deficiencies in one area by exaggerated striving in another area, all of which is destined to lead to a lowered sense of self-esteem.

In discussing adjustment to the uncertainty of rheumatoid arthritis, Wiener (1975) found examples of succumbing behavior.

Borrowing the term "as if" from Wright (1960), she noted that arthritic patients attempt to normalize their situation through "covering up" or "keeping up" strategies. "Covering up" involves hiding the disability or pain from others. "Keeping up" calls for pushing oneself to perform as if one were not suffering from the pain and swelling that interferes with normal activity. Wiener (1975) even noted cases of "super-normalizing," "excessive keeping up on good days" (p. 100). The problem with these "as if" strategies is that they can aggravate the condition, cause other people to be confused about the person's erratic behavior, and lead afflicted individuals to feel that no one understands the nature of their problem.

Signs of Coping

On the other hand, there are signs of coping or positive striving in regard to disability that can be observed (Wright, 1960). For example:

1. Enlarging the scope of values—The individual has an emotional realization that other values are possible and that these values can be realized, even given the limitations of the disability.
2. Containing disability's effects—Learning of new skills and approaches helps the individual overcome limitations of the disability.
3. Acceptance—The disability is accepted as nondevaluating, though limiting and inconveniencing.
4. Subordinating the physique—Shifting undue value on physical competence and normality to personality traits such as kindness, wisdom, and effort, which mean more than outward appearances.
5. Counteracting spread—The individual realizes that not all of life is determined or affected by the disability.
6. Comparative versus asset values—Disabled individuals move away from comparing themselves with external standards (oughts, presumed averages, what other people seem to be able to do) and look at their own personal assets to meet situational demands. Physique is viewed in terms of its inherent characteristics and assets, with an emphasis on utilizing those assets to the maximum.

Supporting Wright's comments on value change and development as a sign of coping, Fogel and Rosillo (1969) found greater goal flexibility in those physical rehabilitation clients who made greater improvement. They concluded that "...high recovery patients tended to have more flexibility in terms of their ability to shift those goals most important to them, such as vocational ambitions, psychological pursuits, recreational outlets, and any other important personal ambitions" (Fogel and Rosillo, p. 597).

Wiener (1975) also discussed renormalization practices used by arthritic patients. For example, she found that many patients made conscious decisions of a pacing nature; i.e., identifying what activities one is able to do, how often, and under what circumstances. Changing almost daily due to the variation in the effect of the condition, pacing decisions include how long to allow to dress, how much work to do per day or week, how much housework to do, etc. Another aspect of this renormalizing had to do with adjusting to reduced activity levels and developing a new set of norms regarding what one can do. Being able to ask for help when it is needed is another step in renormalizing for the arthritic patient. However, these renormalizing activities have some dangerous side effects. For example, the obvious problem with asking for help is that it increases the individual's fear of dependency (Wiener, 1975, p. 101).

Before closing our discussion of adjustment to disability in terms of clinical generalizations, it is important to review some notable exceptions and qualifications. First of all, it should be emphasized that the level of adjustment of disabled clients is generally similar to that of nondisabled persons. However, the research reviews presented in Chapter 2 suggest that there are predictable differences when the average level of adjustment of large samples of disabled persons is objectively assessed.

Several studies illustrate the importance of the predisability personality to adjustment. In a literature review of spinal cord injury studies, Cook (1976) pointed out that extreme responses to spinal cord injury, such as physiological suicide, e.g., ignoring body sores, could be traced to pre-injury personality aberrations. Further, Dobson et al.(1971) noted that the pre-attack personality of the cardiac patient strongly influenced adjustment to myocardial infarction.

In his review, Cook (1976) also reported several studies that questioned the universality of the sequential responses to disability, i.e., denial, mourning, depression, anger, and positive coping. Dinardo (1971) found that deniers made the best adjustment to spinal cord injury and that the absence of depression was related to good adjustment. In a survey of spinal cord injured patients, Mueller (1962) found that approximately 50% of the injured individuals did not experience depression.

Hence, an individual-by-individual approach to adjustment to disability is important. However, generalizations, if they are not blinding, help in providing both an explanation for what one is observing and a framework for a theoretical understanding of adjustment and disability that leads to hypotheses about new ways to serve the disabled. With some caution, one can, for example, apply concepts implicit in the succumbing or coping notions to the development of a model for adjustment to disability.

A MODEL FOR ADJUSTMENT TO DISABILITY

A model for adjustment to disability in rehabilitation must have certain attributes. First, it must focus on the process of person/ situation fit and the way in which disability disrupts that fit. It must be an asset model that emphasizes abilities and not disabilities. It must emphasize skills and behaviors needed by the individual to: 1) contain the effects of the disability, 2) enlarge the scope of values, and 3) avoid eclipsing of behavioral possibilities.

Parts of several adjustment models, as previously discussed, are useful at this point. The survival model, for example, contributes the idea of the importance of the desire to live. The engineering model provides an asset focus that takes into consideration the range of an individual's potential efficiency. The positive striving model provides a value scheme for identifying directions to take for developing skill or behavioral programs. Hence, by bringing the concepts of survival, asset, person/environment fit, and positive striving together with their emphases on the dimensions of process, continuity, operationalization, observation, measurement, and skills or behaviors, one has the foundation for a comprehensive adjustment model for rehabilitation. One label for that comprehensive adjustment model might be "behavioral coping." In a behavioral coping approach, maladjustment is viewed as problems in living, and the preferred treatment involves helping clients identify and learn responses to their situational problems.

A behavioral coping model is concerned with the individual's ability to manage his or her environment with a minimum of discomfort to self and others and a minimum of inefficiency. The model emphasizes training individuals in the skills or behaviors needed for generating positive rewards from the environment while avoiding punishment, or at least excessively high rates of punishment (Adams, 1972). These rewards might span such biologically significant issues as food, water, sex, oxygen, avoidance of pain, etc., and secondary or conditioned rewards such as attention, emotional approval, money, etc. As Trieschmann (1974) pointed out, "The key to coping with one's disability is to receive enough satisfactions and rewards to make life worthwhile" (p. 558). The behavioral coping approach to rehabilitation covers a wide range of activities for adjustment training and meets many of the criteria previously identified as desirable in adjustment models. It is described in greater detail in Chapter 3.

SUMMARY

Personal adjustment training is an area in which rehabilitation clients learn the skills necessary to become productive community members. Two issues in defining adjustment, achievement versus process, and frame of reference, plus several models of adjustment —survival, medical, positive striving, and others—are relevant considerations in defining adjustment to disability. The relationship between psychosocial adjustment and vocational adjustment has not been definitely established; however, the available evidence suggests that they are distinguishable, yet mutually facilitative. Prejudicial attitudes toward disabled persons often constitute a greater barrier to successful adjustment than does the actual disabling condition. The effects of disability on the individual can be conceptualized in terms of three broad classes of responses—restoration, succumbing, and coping. The various concepts and issues outlined in this chapter suggest that a behavioral coping approach to adjustment to disability provides the most suitable model for adjustment training in rehabilitation.

Chapter 2

Disability and Personal Adjustment

Undoubtedly the most researched topic in psychology of disability concerns the effects of disablement on personal adjustment. Is self-esteem diminished as the result of disablement? Does the occurrence of disability lead to severe emotional maladjustment? What effects might disability have on the broad area of normal personality functioning? The relationship between disability and the three aspects of personality referred to in these questions—self-concept, psychopathology, and the normal personality sphere—are considered in detail in this chapter, but first three general conclusions are outlined.

The results of numerous studies (see Barker et al., 1953; McDaniel, 1976; Pringle, 1964; Shontz, 1971; and Wright, 1960) have supported three often-repeated and independently derived conclusions: 1) specific disabilities are not associated with identifiable personality types, e.g., deaf persons are not characterized by a particular personality syndrome, nor are amputees, blind persons, arthritics, etc.; 2) there is no simple relationship between severity of disability and degree of psychological impairment, e.g., quadriplegics are not necessarily less well adjusted than paraplegics and multiple amputees may evidence better adjustment than persons with minor, yet visible, burn injuries; 3) there exists a wide range of individual reactions to disability, e.g., two persons with very similar handicapping conditions often demonstrate entirely different types of response to their situations.

While these conclusions may suggest that much of the research on the personal adjustment of disabled persons has been without value, we believe that there are significant findings of practical importance to rehabilitation practitioners. Consequently, this chapter includes an examination of the research literature that addresses the three questions in the initial paragraph of the chapter. However, it should be emphasized that unique, individual reactions to disability are the norm. Yet, these idiosyncratic responses can be viewed within a broader framework of personal adjustment to disablement. It is the purpose of this chapter to provide that structural framework.

One additional issue that bears on the interpretation of investigations of the personal adjustment of disabled persons requires brief mention. The question of cause and effect, i.e., does disablement cause alterations in personality functioning, or are certain personality characteristics predisposing factors in either the occurrence of disability or the reaction to disablement, can only be answered tentatively with nonexperimental data. The available evidence suggests that both kinds of causal influence occur. Of course, it is the impact of disability on personality functioning and adjustment that is of utmost concern to rehabilitation practitioners.

DISABILITY AND SELF-CONCEPT

The occurrence of disablement may bring changes in the person's appearance, capabilities, and functional skills. It logically follows that the disabled person's view of himself or herself would be altered to accommodate self-perceived physical or mental changes. The extent to which the revised conception of self consists of negative evaluations will most certainly constitute an impediment to successful rehabilitation. This is so not simply because the disabled person's self-esteem is impaired, but because one's perception of self influences one's perception of other's views of oneself, thereby rendering social interaction more difficult. Clearly, then, the study of the relationship between disablement and self-concept is relevant to our understanding of the interpersonal dynamics of the rehabilitation process.

The psychological construct of self-concept is not a new one. In the twentieth century alone, more than half a dozen theorists (James, Cooley, Mead, Lecky, Sullivan, Hilgard, Snygg and Combs, and Rogers) have identified themselves as self-theorists or phenomenologists. Their various positions share the common postulate that a person's view of himself or herself provides the only perspective from which behavior can be understood. Epstein (1973) reviewed the positions of the above-mentioned theorists and summarized the characteristics of the self-concept as follows (p. 407):

1. It is a subsystem of internally consistent, hierarchically organized concepts contained within a broader conceptual system
2. It contains different empirical selves, such as a body self, a spiritual self, and a social self
3. It is a dynamic organization that changes with experience
4. It develops out of experience, particularly out of social interaction with significant others
5. It is essential for the functioning of the individual that the organization of the self-concept be maintained
6. There is a basic need for self-esteem, which relates to all aspects of the self-system
7. The self-concept has at least two basic functions: a) it organizes the data of experience, and b) it facilitates attempts to fulfill needs

Epstein proposed that the self-concept is a self-theory that each individual constructs about himself or herself out of his or her totality of experience. The fundamental purpose of the self-theory is to optimize the pleasure/pain balance of the individual over the course of a lifetime. The overall stability of the individual's self-theory is determined by his or her ability to derive pleasure from life, to assimilate experience, and to maintain self-esteem. A self-theory under minimum threat or stress would include postulates such as "I like myself and consider myself to be a decent person" and "I expect to lead a happy life," while a self-theory under stress, and therefore subject to disorganization, would contain postulates such as "Life is meaningless and has nothing to offer me" and "No one whom I respect could ever care for me."

The terms self-concept, self-image, self-esteem, ego, self-view, etc., are often used interchangeably. For our purposes, these terms and similar ones all refer to an individual's evaluation of himself or herself as a more or less worthy person. Thus, self-concept or self-esteem suggests more than a picture of oneself; it includes the individual's evaluation of the picture as good or bad (or somewhere between these two extremes) and is hypothesized to be relevant to his or her optimal adjustment and functioning.

At this point it would seem appropriate to acknowledge a dissenting point of view. The eminent psychologist J. P. Guilford (1959) made the following statements about the self-concept:

> The concept of *self* is of special interest in personality study. Some writers refer to the *ego*, some use both terms, but no two authors agree fully on the use of either term. ... It is the author's view that in a well-

developed theory of behavior or of personality, the concepts of self and ego will have little place. ... The worst thing that can be said about either concept is that it comes dangerously close to animism—the "little-man-within-the-outer-man" idea, which is quite foreign to science (Guilford, p. 27).

Research Review

While several standard textbooks in rehabilitation psychology contain detailed discussions of the impact of disablement on self-concept and the process of reorganization of the self-system during the rehabilitation process (e.g., Safilios-Rothschild, 1970, pp. 93–109; Wright, 1960, pp. 138–178), few empirical investigations are cited to support the conclusions reached. Most data are found in autobiographical accounts and clinical case studies. The majority of the studies summarized in the following paragraphs have been reported in doctoral theses and constitute the core of the empirical evidence bearing on the relationships among disablement, self-concept, and rehabilitation success.

In an early study, Fishman (1949) concluded that an amputee's adjustment to a leg prosthesis is dependent, to a considerable degree, upon his self-concept, although this was by no means the only determining factor. Shelsky (1957) compared the retrospective, present, and ideal self-perceptions of samples of amputees, and tuberculous, and acutely ill patients. The results indicated that the type of disability differentially affects the self-concept, with tuberculosis having the greater negative impact. Smits (1964) assessed the self-concepts of a sample of disabled high school students and concluded that severely disabled adolescents have significantly lower self-concept scores than adolescents whose physical disabilities are mild, with severely disabled females most negatively affected. Meissner (1966) also studied disabled adolescents, but her findings were not as clear-cut as those of Smits; however, she did find that severely disabled females had significantly lower self-concepts than other females.

Meighan (1970) administered the Tennessee Self Concept Scale (TSCS) to a sample of visually handicapped (blind and partially sighted) adolescents and found that their self-concepts were extremely low compared with the norm group. However, a study by Williams (1971) that compared a sample of blind adolescents using Bill's High School Index of Adjustment and Values produced the opposite result: blind subjects reported significantly higher self-concepts.

Schurr, Joiner, and Towne (1970) reviewed the self-concept research with mentally retarded subjects published prior to 1970 and concluded that differences in subject samples and instrumentation, as well as inconsistent results (some studies found no differences between retarded and normal persons while others reported lower self-concepts for the retarded) precluded any generalizations about the typical mentally retarded person's self-concept. In an investigation that was published after the Schurr, Joiner, and Towne review was completed, Collins, Burger, and Doherty (1970) compared an educable mentally retarded (EMR) sample and a sample of nonretarded adolescents using the TSCS. The retarded subjects were significantly lower on several self-concept variables than the nonretarded subjects, and both groups were below the norm group.

The greatest consensus among independent studies has been achieved with alcoholics. Mathias (1955) investigated the personality structure of chronic alcoholics from a psychoanalytic perspective and concluded that they have marked needs for submission and self-debasement. Gross and Alder (1970) administered the TSCS to a sample of male alcoholics, who reported lower self-concepts than the norm sample and who were more self-critical. Hall (1973) studied active and recovered alcoholics using the TSCS and found that, while recovered alcoholics indicated normal levels of self-esteem, those of active alcoholics were significantly lower.

Fitts (1972a) reported the results of a large-scale investigation of 1,754 psychiatric patients using the Tennessee Self Concept Scale. He reviewed other studies of the self-concepts of various psychiatric samples and drew the following conclusions: psychotic patients have "very disturbed, deviant self-concepts" (p. 43), psychoneurotics "tend to have low self-esteem" (p. 60), "the alcoholic does not like, respect, or value himself" (p. 87), and "mental retardates may have lower self-esteem" (p. 97). However, with regard to the last group, Fitts noted that the TSCS may not be a valid measure with retarded subjects (p. 98).

In a subsequent monograph, Fitts (1972b) stated that

A general overview of the data from a number of handicapped populations (orthopedic handicaps, cleft palate, the deaf, the blind, severe kidney disorders, Hansen's disease, cerebral palsy, and others) indicates that physical disabilities are seemingly less related to the self-concept than psychiatric disabilities (pp. 32–33).

He speculated that while

The state of knowledge on the relationship between self-concept and disability is quite limited ... this should be a rich area for additional research. I would predict that many revealing relationships will be demonstrated. As other variables are adequately controlled, it seems likely that the differential effects of type of disorder and severity of disorder will be reflected in self-concept. A more likely discovery may be that self-concept differences *within* disability groups will have the same significance as they do in any population (Fitts, 1972b, p. 34).

In summary, the available evidence suggests two conclusions: 1) disabled persons report lower self-esteem than nondisabled persons, and 2) some disabling conditions have greater impact on self-concept than others. The data supporting the second conclusion are much more tenuous than those that support the first, because few studies have directly compared the self-concepts of persons with different types of disabilities. Furthermore, differences in instrumentation and subject samples, several of which were comprised of institutionalized adolescents, render comparisons across investigations more difficult.

DISABILITY AND PSYCHOPATHOLOGY

Popular belief, some personality theories, and the results of numerous psychometric studies suggest that there is a relationship between disablement and psychological maladjustment. While the evidence supporting the association is usually methodologically weak and often contradictory, the presumed correlation between disability and emotional disturbance is difficult to dismiss. This is so, in part, because the notion is intuitively appealing; furthermore, several reasonably sound studies have provided positive support for the hypothesized relationship. A confounding factor is the rejecting attitude held by many nondisabled persons toward the disabled. In fact, as discussed in Chapter 1, the stigma of disability may exert a more profound influence on the psychological adjustment of disabled persons than the various direct effects of the physical, mental, or emotional impairments.

The vast majority of studies that have attempted to assess the relationship between disability and psychopathology have entailed the administration of the Minnesota Multiphasic Personality Inventory (MMPI) to a sample of persons with a particular disability. The studies usually include an extended discussion of the disabled group profile as it compares to the MMPI norm group. Due mainly to the idiosyncrasies of sample selection, most of these investigations are not comparable and thus cannot be used as the basis for definitive conclusions regarding the relative psychological adjustments among disabling conditions. The interested reader is referred to Lanyon (1968) and Shontz (1970, 1971) for summaries of the MMPI studies and similar studies using other instruments, and to Buros (1975) for the most comprehensive MMPI bibliography available.

Research Review

Two large multisample investigations of disabling conditions using the MMPI have been reported in the psychological literature. They are reviewed in some detail in this section: first, a typical MMPI disability study and then, for contrast, a methodologically unique study involving four disability groups are briefly summarized.

De Cencio, Leshner, and Leshner (1968) analyzed the average MMPI profile of 43 medical patients with a primary diagnosis of chronic obstructive pulmonary emphysema (COPE). The mean scores on nine of the ten clinical scales were significantly higher than those of the norm group, with scores on the neurotic triad (Hypochondriasis, Depression, and Hysteria) being substantially elevated. When compared to three disability groups from a previously reported study conducted by other investigators, the COPE sample was significantly lower on several scales and higher on some others. The authors interpreted the pattern of differences among groups as providing some support for the hypothesis that specific personality factors may be associated with different disabilities (De Cencio, Leshner, and Leshner, 1968, p. 474).

An investigation by Vernier, Stafford, and Krugman (1958) compared four disability groups (orthopedic, respiratory, cardiac, and neurologic) using 29 scores obtained from four projective tests (Bender-Gestalt, Rorschach, DAP, and Rhode-Hildreth Sentence Completion). Although the results of a factor analysis produced some modest correlations between disability groups and personality factors, the authors concluded that the pattern of loadings "... would be consistent with the theory that personality variables are not associated with specific types of physical disease" (Vernier, Stafford, and Krugman, 1958, p. 436).

In addition to illustrating different measurement and statistical approaches to the question of the relationship between personality maladjustment and type of disability, these two studies demonstrate the need for representative samples of disabled subjects. Of course, the contrasting conclusions drawn from the studies are not unusual in the psychological literature, and reflect the orientations and biases of the authors as much as anything else. The results of the large-scale investigations summarized next do help to clarify the nature and extent of the disability-psychopathology relationship.

Almost 30 years ago, Wiener (1948) reported MMPI data for five categories of disabled Veteran's Administration (VA) counseling clients: arthritis, asthma, gunshot wounds, malaria, and ulcers. Each of the disabled samples was compared to a nondisabled sample drawn from the same population (young male World War II veterans). The mean profiles of the disability groups were different from the nondisabled profile on one or more MMPI scales; these results were used to summarize the unique psychopathological characteristics of each disability. While the author did not so state, the implication is that the data support a relationship between type of disability and nature of maladjustment.

The most comprehensive study in the literature was conducted by Warren and Weiss (1969). They evaluated both the dimensional and typological hypotheses using MMPI scores of rehabilitation clients representing nine disability categories and a nondisabled sample. Five of the groups were physically disabled (arthritis, epilepsy, heart disease, orthopedic impairment–back, and orthopedic impairment–lower limbs) and four included mental disorders (mental retardation and psychoneurotic, schizophrenic, and character disorders). ANOVA comparisons on nine MMPI clinical scales (Masculinity/Femininity was excluded) and the L and F validity scales were statistically significant at the 0.01 level. Furthermore, the mean t-score range for the clinical scales was 17.1, indicating that the average separation between highest and lowest scoring groups was more than one and a half standard deviations. All groups except lower limb orthopedic impairment and character disorders had t-score means elevated at least one standard deviation on the neurotic triad. Psychopathic Deviate scale means were similarly elevated for all groups except heart disease. The Paranoia, Psychasthenia, and Schizophrenia scales showed a different pattern. These scales differentiated four groups whose scores were elevated more than the other groups: schizophrenic disorders, psychoneurotic disorders, mental retardation, and epilepsy.

In contrast to the significant dimensional differences noted above, the typological analysis did not produce the predicted results. When ten clusters composed of clients with similar MMPI profiles were examined, no consistent tendency was found for persons with the same disability to cluster together. In conclusion, support was found for the dimensional hypothesis that disability groups can be differentiated on the basis of individual MMPI scales. No support, however, was found for the hypothesis that there are MMPI profile types that correspond to disability groups.

DISABILITY AND THE NORMAL PERSONALITY SPHERE

The Sixteen Personality Factor Questionnaire (16PF) was developed and refined over a period of several decades beginning in the early 1940s (Cattell, 1946, 1957, 1973). It purports to measure the 16 primary source traits that explain interpersonal variation in normal personality functioning. The factorial validity of the 16PF with rehabilitation clients was established in two recently reported investigations (Bolton, 1977a; Burdsal and Bolton, in press). The interested reader is referred to the *Eighth Mental Measurements Yearbook* review by Bolton (1978a), which concluded that "when evaluated by reasonable standards, the 16PF compares favorably with any other inventory that purports to measure variations in normal personality functioning."

Research Review

The 16PF has been used in more than two dozen empirical investigations of the personality characteristics of a broad range of physically and psychiatrically disabling conditions. Following brief reviews of the individual studies, the salient profile characteristics (high and low scores) of 19 samples of disabled persons are summarized and examined for possible generalized effects of disablement. To facilitate comparability among the studies reviewed, a standard vocabulary was used to summarize the results of each study. The brief bipolar trait descriptors that were employed are contained in Table 1.

Physical Disabilities   Two studies reported in the psychological literature assessed the relationship between general physical illness and personality. Stewart (1965) compared the 16PF profiles of 47 student nurses (all females) who reported a low frequency of physical illness and 28 who reported a high frequency of illness. The "illness" group scored higher on L (suspicious), N (shrewd), and Q_4 (tense), and lower on C (emotionally less stable).

Using a longitudinal design, Barton and Cattell (1972) studied 593 New Zealand high school seniors who completed the 16PF at age 18 and five years later at age 23. The personality scores of

Table 1. Brief descriptions of the sixteen personality source traits measured by the 16PF[a]

Trait	Low scores =	High scores =
A	Reserved	Outgoing
B	Less intelligent	More intelligent
C	Emotionally less stable	Emotionally stable
E	Submissive	Assertive
F	Sober	Enthusiastic
G	Expedient	Conscientious
H	Shy	Venturesome
I	Realistic	Sensitive
L	Trusting	Suspicious
M	Conventional	Imaginative
N	Forthright	Shrewd
O	Confident	Apprehensive
Q_1	Conservative	Liberal
Q_2	Group-dependent	Self-sufficient
Q_3	Undisciplined	Controlled
Q_4	Relaxed	Tense

[a] Detailed descriptions of the 16 source traits are presented in Chapter 9 of the *Handbook for the Sixteen Personality Factor Questionnaire* (Cattell, Eber, and Tatsuoka, 1970).

148 subjects who reported a chronic illness during the five-year interval were compared with those of the 445 subjects who reported no serious illness. A two-way analysis of variance indicated that the "illness" sample scored higher on O (apprehensive) and Q_4 (tense), and lower on C (emotionally less stable).

The relationship between physically handicapping conditions and personality in college students was examined by Tucker (1968). Fifty-seven physically handicapped students were compared to 505 non-handicapped students. The handicapped sample scored higher on B (more intelligent) and M (imaginative), and lower on F (sober). These differences would suggest that selection factors related to college attendance had more impact than the presence of a disability per se.

Three investigations were concerned with specific disabling conditions other than heart disease. Kirchman (1965) compared the 16PF scores of 25 rheumatoid arthritic patients to those of 25 non-arthritic physically disabled patients and to the 16PF general population standardization sample. While there were no statistically significant differences between the arthritic and disabled samples, there were five significant differences between the arthritic sample and the general population. The arthritic sample was higher on M (imaginative), Q_3 (controlled), and Q_4 (tense), and lower on E (submissive) and F (sober).

Phillip and Cay (1972) studied 25 patients with the diagnosis of peptic ulcers and 43 patients with other diseases of the gastro-intestinal system. There were no significant differences between the 16PF profiles of the two groups. However, when the combined group of 68 patients was compared to a sample of 284 normal adults, the following differences were revealed: the patients were higher on Q_2 (self-sufficient), and lower on C (emotionally less stable) and H (shy). The authors interpreted this pattern to "...suggest a turning of attention towards the self and away from other oriented activity" (Phillip and Cay, p. 49).

Comparisons between a sample of 68 asthmatics selected at random from registers of known cases and the sample of 284 normal adults were reported by Rosenthal, Aitken, and Zeally (1973). The asthmatics were higher on Q_1 (liberal), and lower on E (submissive) and I (realistic). There was little support for any relationship between severity of asthmatic condition and personality factors. The authors concluded that "there is little or no evidence for the existence of a specific 'asthmatic personality' " (Rosenthal, Aitken, and Zeally, p. 13). They did note, however, that in individual cases personality characteristics may intensify the emotional reaction to the disorder.

Hypertension is somewhat unique as a systemic arterial disease: afflicted persons may not become aware of the presence of the condition until its consequences are realized in the form of a serious disablement, e.g., kidney malfunction, stroke, heart attack, etc. Thus, hypertensive patients constitute a special group for the investigation of psychosomatic/somatopsychological relationships. Kidson (1973) compared the 16PF profiles of 60 male hypertensive outpatients and 110 non-patient males selected from an industrial organization. The hypertensive patients were significantly higher on O (apprehensive) and Q_4 (tense), and lower on B (less intelligent), C (emotionally less stable), M (conventional), and Q_1 (conservative). The author conjectured that sample differences in age and social class may have partially accounted for the differences on B, M, and Q_1, but that the differences on C, O, and Q_4 were evidence of an anxiety reaction to hypertension.

Three 16PF investigations of male patients suffering from

coronary heart disease are contained in the literature. The earliest study compared 36 patients who had suffered myocardial infarction with 42 control subjects with no signs of cardiovascular disease after appropriate examinations (Miles et al., 1954). The coronary patients were higher on A (outgoing), F (enthusiastic), O (apprehensive), and Q_4 (tense), and lower on B (less intelligent), C (emotionally less stable), and N (forthright).

Bakker (1967) studied 112 patients suffering from arteriosclerotic heart disease, 52 of whom were diagnosed with angina pectoris. Patients with and without angina were compared within age, education, and vocational groups. Several consistent differences were found in the older, lower socio-economic subgroups: angina pectoris patients were higher on O (apprehensive), and lower on C (emotionally less stable), E (submissive), and G (expedient).

Shekelle and Ostfeld (1965) carried out a prospective study of the relationship between personality factors and coronary heart disease that began with the administration of the 16PF to an initial sample of 1,990 men between 40 and 55 years of age who were free of coronary symptoms. After four years had elapsed, 31 cases of angina pectoris and 18 cases of myocardial infarction had occurred. Several results are noteworthy: 1) the angina sample scored significantly lower than the infarction sample on C (emotionally less stable), supporting the finding in Bakker's investigation; 2) both the angina and infarct samples scored higher than the coronary-free group on L (suspicious) and Q_2 (self-sufficient); 3) in comparison to the general population norms, the coronary patients were higher on M (imaginative), O (apprehensive), and Q_2 (self-sufficient), and lower on C (less emotionally stable), E (submissive), and F (sober).

It should be noted that Chapter 14 of the *Handbook for the Sixteen Personality Factor Questionnaire* (*Handbook for the 16PF*) (Cattell, Eber, and Tatsuoka, 1970) presents the 16PF profiles for several additional physically disabled samples: hearing impaired, visually handicapped, epileptic, tuberculous, locomotor impaired, and speech disordered persons. Because most of the data were previously unpublished, sampling procedures were not specified and significance tests were not reported, the results are not included here. The interested reader is referred to the *Handbook* for details.

Psychiatric Disabilities The 16PF profiles for two general categories of emotional disablement are summarized by Cattell, Eber, and Tatsuoka (1970). In comparison to the general population norms, a sample of 272 male and female neurotics was higher on I (sensitive), L (suspicious), O (apprehensive), and Q_4 (tense), and lower on C (emotionally less stable), E (submissive), F (sober), G (expedient), H (shy), and Q_3 (undisciplined). A sample of 531 male and female psychotics was higher on O (apprehensive) and lower on B (less intelligent), C (emotionally less stable), and L (trusting). The personality profiles for numerous psychiatric diagnostic groups are presented in Chapter 14 of the *Handbook for the 16PF*. Only selected data are included here, because of the wide availability of the *Handbook for the 16PF*, and because of the reasons given above.

Three studies of schizophrenic patients have been reported. Cattell, Komlos, and Tatro (1968) administered the 16PF to 125 male and female psychotics during the first week after hospital admission. When compared to two control groups, the psychotic sample was higher on A (outgoing), O (apprehensive), Q_2 (self-sufficient), and Q_3 (controlled), and lower on C (emotionally less stable), E (submissive), F (sober), and H (shy).

A sample of 69 male and female chronic hospitalized schizophrenics completed the 16PF in conjunction with an investigation by Gleser and Gottschalk (1967). Compared to the general population norms, the schizophrenics were higher on A (outgoing), O (apprehensive), and Q_2 (self-sufficient), and lower on B (less intelligent), C (emotionally less stable), F (sober), G (expedient), and H (shy). These differences stemmed primarily from the male sub-sample.

The reader will note that the results of the two independent studies of schizophrenics described above are very similar, suggesting the possibility of a general schizophrenic personality profile. However, the third investigation did not confirm this pattern. Serban and Katz (1975) administered Form E of the 16PF to 515 schizophrenic patients admitted to the Bellevue Psychiatric Hospital. The research sample scored significantly higher than the population norms on 14 of 16 scales; there was no difference on Q_3 and the schizophrenics were lower on G (expedient). The authors concluded that the validity of Form E with schizophrenics is questionable.

Alcoholics have been extensively studied by psychologists. Four investigations using the 16PF are summarized below. DePalma and Clayton (1958) analyzed the 16PF scores of 69 male alcoholics hospitalized for treatment by court order. In comparison to the general population norms, the alcoholics were higher on I (sensitive) and

Q_3 (controlled), and lower on B (less intelligent) and F (sober).

Gross and Carpenter (1971) administered the 16PF to 266 male alcoholics at the time of their admission to a VA hospital treatment program. Compared to the general norms, the alcoholics were higher on A (outgoing), B (more intelligent), L (suspicious), M (imaginative), O (apprehensive), and Q_4 (tense), and lower on C (emotionally less stable), E (submissive), G (expedient), H (shy), N (forthright), and Q_1 (conservative). The authors concluded that the data support the view that chronic alcoholics are a distinct personality type.

In conjunction with a study of group psychotherapy (Hoy, 1969), 75 alcoholic patients in a hospital treatment program completed the 16PF at the time of admission. Compared to the population norms, the alcoholic sample scored higher on B (more intelligent), L (suspicious), O (apprehensive), and Q_4 (tense), and lower on C (emotionally less stable), G (expedient), and H (shy).

Kirchner and Marzolf (1974) compared the 16PF scores of 49 male alcoholics who were participating in an inpatient treatment program to the 16PF standardization sample. The alcoholics were higher on B (more intelligent), I (sensitive), L (suspicious), O (apprehensive), and Q_4 (tense), and lower on A (reserved), C (emotionally less stable), F (sober), G (expedient), H (shy), Q_2 (group-dependent), and Q_3 (controlled).

Other Studies   Several investigations reported in the literature, in addition to the 16PF profiles summarized in the *Handbook for the 16PF* that were previously noted, were not included in the preceding review. Specific reasons for omission varied, but they all pertained to the crucial issue of data dependability. In the interest of comprehensiveness, the excluded studies are briefly described in this section. Golightly and Reinehr (1969) compared the 16PF profiles of 59 male alcoholics to six criterion groups: 64% of the sample were classified as "neurotic." Brien, Kleiman, and Eisenman (1972) compared four subject samples: heroin users, alcoholics, methedrine users, and mixed users. All subjects were from lower socio-economic backgrounds.

Two recent articles (Trybus, 1973; Jensema, 1975) report analyses of 16PF-E data for deaf college students. The use of Form E, which was constructed for low-literacy adults, with college students is questionable, even recognizing that deaf persons are often educationally retarded. Dunn (1969) administered the 16PF-E to a small sample of spinal cord injured patients as part of the evaluation of a theoretical model of adjustment to disability. Muhlern (1975) administered the 16PF-E to a very small sample of young adult retardates and concluded that "...the extension of this instrument to the study of the mentally retarded is both feasible and useful" (p. 28).

Conclusions The results of the 19 selected 16PF studies of physically and psychiatrically disabled persons are summarized in Table 2. The salient characteristics of the 16PF profile for each research sample are indicated in the table by plus (+) symbols, designating higher mean scores, and negative (−) symbols, designating lower mean scores. Thus, Table 2 provides a capsule overview of the pattern of personality source traits that characterize the various disability groups.

Before the discussion of the results of the studies, several factors that mitigate against a synthesis of the findings are outlined here.

1. Design differences—While the majority of the studies included the comparison of a disabled sample to the 16PF population norms, several investigations were limited to the use of "control" groups. For example, Tucker (1968) compared physically handicapped college students and non-handicapped students, and Bakker (1967) compared coronary heart disease patients with and without angina.

2. Different norms—In addition to the different norm groups that were used in developing the standard score conversions for the five forms of the 16PF, two of the investigations employed a comparison group comprised of "284 normal Scottish adults," viz., Phillip and Cay (1972) and Rosenthal, Aitken, and Zeally (1973).

3. Different forms of the 16PF—While most of the 19 studies used Forms A or B, some did use one of the shorter forms (C or D), or Form E, which was developed for use with low-level readers. These five forms were constructed to be interchangeable (parallel) measures of the 16 personality source traits; however, the available evidence is far from convincing (see Table 2.3 on page 12 of the *Manual for the 16PF* (Institute for Personality and Ability Testing, 1972).

4. Sample differences—In addition to the unique characteristics of the research samples that are intended, i.e., the particular physical or psychiatric disability, there are usually unintended (or confounding) characteristics, e.g., age, socio-economic class, education, race, etc. The problem is that these "irrelevant" correlated factors may account for some of the observed person-

Table 2. Nineteen disability investigations using the 16PF[a]

Type of disability	Characteristic personality source traits[b]															
	A	B	C	E	F	G	H	I	L	M	N	O	Q₁	Q₂	Q₃	Q₄
Physical disabilities																
Physical illness			−						+		+	+				+
Chronic illness			−													+
Physical handicap		+			−					+		+				+
Arthritis				−	−					+					+	
Gastrointestinal			−				−						+	+		
Asthma				−				−					+			
Hypertension	+	−	−									+	−			++
Coronary disease		−	−		+	−				−	−	+				++
Coronary disease			−	−		−						+				
Coronary disease			−	−	−					+		+		+		
Psychiatric disabilities																
General neuroticism			−	−	−	−	−	+	+			+			−	+
General psychoticism		−	−	−	−	−	−		−		−	+				
Schizophrenia	+	−	−	+	−	−	−					+		+	+	
Schizophrenia	++	+	−	+	+	−	−			+	+	+		++		
Schizophrenia	+	+	+	+	+	−	+	++	+	+	+	+	+	++		+
Alcoholism	+	−		−	−	−	−	++	+	+						
Alcoholism		+	−			−	−		+	+		+	−		+	+++
Alcoholism		+	−		−	−	−		++		−	+		−		+++
Alcoholism	−	+			−			+						−	−	

[a]The 19 studies are listed in the same order as in the discussion in the text. The Serban and Katz (1975) study is included here, in the interest of objective reporting, even though the authors questioned the validity of the results.
[b]Higher mean scores are designated by a +; lower mean scores are designated by a −.

ality differences (see the reviews of the studies by Tucker (1968) and Kidson (1973)). The unintended differences or correlated factors usually reflect naturally occurring variations associated with the particular disabling condition. Furthermore, some investigations are restricted to subpopulations of especial interest, e.g., male coronary patients or hospitalized male alcoholics.

5. Sample heterogeneity—Most available evidence suggests that there exists as much variation in personality traits within disability groups as in the general population. If this within-group variation could be partitioned or allocated to homogeneous subgroups within disability groups, more precise comparisons among disability groups would be possible. There is evidence that personality subgroups are, in fact, identifiable within the standard disability classifications, e.g., Bolton (1972), Lawlis and Rubin (1971), Nerviano and Gross (1973). A related issue is that of statistically significant differences versus magnitude of observed differences: in general, as sample size increases, smaller differences are detected as "significant." Thus, the absolute size of significant differences varies across studies.

With these cautionary remarks in mind, the data abstracted in Table 2 can be examined for generalized and disability-specific correlates in the realm of the normal personality sphere. To facilitate comprehension of the personality patterns that typify the two major categories of disabilities (physical and psychiatric), as well as disablement generally, the 19 sample profiles have been further collapsed in Table 3.

Four conclusions can be stated. First, the general effect of disablement, which includes physical and psychiatric evidence in about equal proportions, suggests the following personality correlates (in order of magnitude, as reflected by the number of studies in which the difference was observed): emotionally less stable (C^-), apprehensive (O^+), tense (Q_4^+), submissive (E^-), sober (F^-), imaginative (M^+), and self-sufficient (Q_2^+). Scattered differences occurred on N and Q_1, but there was no consistent trend in the data.

Second, *in addition to* the generalized effect, the following differences tended to characterize the psychiatric disabilities: expedient (G^-), shy (H^-), suspicious (L^+), sensitive (I^+), and outgoing (A^+). Several differences were observed on B and Q_3, but were significant in both directions for various samples.

Third, there are no additional effects, beyond the general disablement profile, that are associated with the physical disabilities.

Table 3. Summary of nineteen disability investigations[a]

Type of disability	Occurrences of characteristic personality source traits															
	A	B	C	E	F	G	H	I	L	M	N	O	Q$_1$	Q$_2$	Q$_3$	Q$_4$
Physical disabilities																
Higher (+)	1	1			1				1	3	1	5	1	2	1	5
Lower (−)		2	7	4	3	1	1	1		1	1		1			
Psychiatric disabilities																
Higher (+)	4	4	1	1	1		1	4	5	2	1	8	1	3	2	5
Lower (−)	1	3	7	3	5	6	6	1	1	1	1		1	1	2	
All disabilities																
Higher (+)	5	5	1	1	2		1	4	6	5	2	13	2	5	3	10
Lower (−)	1	5	14	7	8	7	7	1	1	1	2		2	1	2	

[a]The values in this table were obtained by summing the data in the respective columns of Table 2 for the physical and psychiatric disabilities separately, and for the entire set of 19 studies.

And fourth, there do not appear to be any consistent disability-specific effects that extend beyond the general or psychiatric profile patterns. However, only coronary disease, schizophrenia, and alcoholism are sufficiently well represented to justify any conclusions.

Using the well-replicated second-order personality dimensions of the 16PF (Cattell, 1973, Chapter 4), these results can be viewed within a systematically organized framework of reaction to disability. The three traits that best characterize disablement generally (C^-, O^+, and Q_4^+) are the primary contributors to the second-order factor, Anxiety. Within the subset of psychiatric disabilities, two additional factors (H^- and L^+) are additional elements in the broader personality pattern of Anxiety. Thus, the predominant personality response associated with the occurrence of physical and emotional disability is increased anxiety.

The remaining primary source traits that characterized the disability samples do not fall as clearly into second-order patterns; in fact, some of the observed differences appear to be contradictory. This result suggests that Eysenck's (1972) argument, that the primary trait measurements have little meaning beyond what is available in the broader secondary patterns, may be fallacious. The following relationships between observed primary differences and secondary patterns seem reasonable: Q_2^+ is uniquely affiliated (negatively) with the secondary Exvia; A^+, I^+, and M^+ are the primary components (reversed) of the secondary dimension Cortertia; E^-, F^-, and H^- are component elements (reversed) of Independence; and G^- is the major trait (again reversed) comprising Good Upbringing or Super-ego Strength (Cattell, Eber, and Tatsuoka, 1970, Chapter 10).

In summary, the careful examination of the profile characteristics of the 19 disabled samples, considered in the broader context of the 16PF second-order structure, suggests that the following personality manifestations may be observed in disabled persons:

1. A tendency toward introversion (Invia) and self-sufficiency, although some psychiatric disabilities foster an outgoing orientation
2. Increased anxiety, specifically lower ego-strength, greater apprehension, and higher ergic tension; with psychiatric disabilities, the possibility of withdrawal and suspicion
3. A tendency to a mood level of frustration and depression (Pathemia), especially with the psychiatrically disabled
4. A tendency to become more subdued, with decreased evidence of independent functioning

5. Lowered super-ego strength, especially with psychiatrically disabled persons

It should be stressed that these conclusions are based on aggregate data. Therefore, while the general trends are highly reliable, the specific conclusions are only suggestive of the possible effects of disablement on the individual. The nature of reaction to disability is a unique personal response that results from the interaction of pre-disability personality, the meaning of loss, and other idiosyncratic circumstances of the individual case.

SUMMARY

The vast literature on disability and personality supports three general conclusions: specific disabilities are not associated with identifiable personality types, there is no simple relationship between severity of disability and degree of psychological impairment, and there exists a wide range of individual reactions to disability. However, these conclusions, which pertain to individual reactions to disability, can be viewed within a broader framework of personal adjustment to disability that is based on a synthesis of several dozen objective investigations. These studies have been organized under three areas: self-concept, psyschopathology, and the normal personality sphere. A variety of investigations suggest that, on the average, disabled persons report lower self-esteem than nondisabled persons. Thus, disabled persons' views of themselves may mitigate against successful rehabilitation, unless modified through adjustment training. The intuitively appealing notion that the occurrence of disablement leads to serious emotional maladjustment has been addressed by numerous studies; however, the complexity of the hypothesized relationship, and difficulties associated with the interpretation of the most-often used instrument, the MMPI, render any conclusions suspect. Yet, the results of two comparative investigations suggest that different disability groups can be differentiated on the basis of individual MMPI scales. The most convincing empirical evidence concerning the relationship between disability and personality has been produced by investigations using the Sixteen Personality Factor Questionnaire (16PF), an instrument that spans the range of normal personality functioning. The results of 19 studies suggest that disabled persons may manifest tendencies toward introversion, anxiety, frustration and depression, subduedness, and reduced super-ego strength.

Chapter 3

The Behavioral Coping Model

Adjustment services in rehabilitation enhance the individual's capacity to cope with disability-related problems. This pragmatic and functional purpose has led to the development of a wide variety of adjustment services. According to Baker and Sawyer (1971), "The content of activities related to adjustment programs varies a great deal among rehabilitation facilities with some facilities providing work experiences of various kinds while others use group counseling, personal hygiene classes, or activities of daily living programs as the core of their adjustment programs" (p. 2).

The problem with adjustment services in rehabilitation is not so much the heterogeneity of the training activities as it is the fact that too little attention is given to the conceptual or theoretical issues underlying the services. We believe that a consistent position regarding adjustment training is possible. Although reflecting the points of view of different authors, the following statements merge into an integrated definition of adjustment training:

1. "Adjustment services are viewed as enabling the person to learn the behaviors and skills necessary to become a more fully functioning member of the community"(Baker and Sawyer, 1971, p. v).
2. "The emphasis is on the development of effective means of coping with life problems as they unfold in the social context" (Wahler, Delbridge, and Clubb, 1969, p. 124).
3. "The focus is on what people do in relation to the psychological conditions in which they do it" (Mischel, 1973, p. 265).
4. "The desired outcome is that effective behaviors will lead to increases in positive reinforcement from the environment and from the self without increases in rates of punishment" (Adams, 1972, p. 18).

41

5. "A considerable amount of the rehabilitation process can be considered to be a learning situation. The disabled patient must learn new ways of behaving and new methods of responding that will take the place of behavior precluded by the disability" (Trotter and Inman, 1968, p. 347).
6. "Learning the physical-medical aspects of life as a disabled person and learning new activities that are rewarding are the core of the rehabilitation process" (Trieschmann, 1974, p. 556).

ELEMENTS OF AN ADJUSTMENT MODEL

Each of the quoted points of view emphasizes a learning or behavioral orientation that is consistent with the criteria of adjustment outlined in Chapter 1. By definition, the behavioral orientation to adjustment services is a process notion, because it emphasizes responding to a succession of situations. Adjustment is not viewed as a state that, once reached, is forever ensured.

The behavioral orientation can also be operationalized so that the points of view of the individual and of the rehabilitation professional are considered in making decisions regarding needed behavior changes. Not always something imposed on a person by an external agent, behavior change can represent a set of mutually arrived at decisions regarding competencies needed to cope more effectively with "problems in living."

Another strength of the behavioral orientation is that it is based on observable criteria. The approach requires moving away from ambiguous goals, such as actualization, self-confidence, independence, and personal adequacy, to behaviors serving as signs of the accomplishment of higher order abstractions. Adjustment services deal with the observable, measurable behaviors and skills an individual can acquire.

Implicit within the behavioral approach is cultural relativity. According to Baker and Sawyer (1971), clients must learn that cultural relativity means that they may have to adapt to two cultures—the values of an immediate community and its subcultures, and the values of the workplace with its different subculture.

At the same time, the concept of cultural relativity does not serve as an excuse for a lack of clearly defined goals on the part of client and counselor. Objectives such as those identified in the positive striving model can guide the approach to adjustment services. For example, the positive striving model emphasizes: 1) positive self-regard, 2) self-awareness, 3) self-actualization, 4) autonomy, and 5) environmental mastery (Sechrest and Wallace, 1967). Such abstract values require operationalization into behavioral terms so that practitioners working in the adjustment area can know what to do to enhance client self-actualization and autonomy.

Of equal importance, it must be recognized that each individual is unique. Individuals differ in terms of behavioral deficits and surpluses that result in behavioral problems requiring an individualized approach to diagnosis and treatment. Individual differences exist also in the extent to which individuals can master new behaviors and coping skills, i.e., adoption of behavioral skills requires practice over a long period of reinforcement.

In essence, personal adjustment training services should focus on helping clients develop effective means of coping with problems in living. The actual content of adjustment services must be specified in terms of behaviors and actions that are recognized as beneficial by both counselor and client. In some cases, these behaviors and skills are adopted because they are necessary for success in one subculture of importance to the client and, in other cases, because they pertain to another subculture of importance. In all, the behavioral coping skills are aimed at helping others see that the individual is developing in autonomy and self-actualization.

A THEORY FOR ADJUSTMENT SERVICES

Theoretical support for the coping and behavioral skill approach to adjustment services is subsumed in an approach to human development stressing cognitive social learning principles (Mischel, 1968, 1973). Because of its emphasis on the centrality of person/environment interaction, the cognitive social learning model has many applications for rehabilitation adjustment services. It provides a theoretical underpinning for understanding human behavior. It suggests ways in which individuals can change their behavior. Philosophically, the cognitive social learning position is consistent with the approach to adjustment services that stresses responding to life's problems. Indeed, using cognitive social learning principles, one can develop responses to the client problems most often encountered in rehabilitation (Fordyce, 1971):

1. Retaining behavioral characteristics that are incompatible with what the individual is now capable of doing

2. Coping with a sudden onset of crisis with a tendency to anticipate disastrous consequences of the new state
3. Acquiring effective behaviors not previously in the person's repertoire

The cognitive social learning approach emphasizes assessment of behavior in the context in which it occurs. The context includes both person and environmental variables, subsumed in the following four-step process: stimuli, person, behavior, and consequences. The basic premise underlying this sequence is that behavior is a function of a stimulus, a person, and a consequence. For example, stimuli or cues elicit either conditioned reactions (the sight of a snake causing a fear reaction) or operant behaviors (behaviors designed to gain rewards or to avoid punishments). The stimuli may be internal or external, in the sense that the person might have certain thoughts or feelings (internal) associated with certain behaviors, or that qualities of the environment (external) might be associated with certain behaviors.

The empty organism position is rejected in the interaction philosophy of cognitive social learning theory; certain person variables are posited as mediators of individual action. According to Mischel (1973), individual differences can be attributed to the following person variables:

1. Construction competencies: the ability to generate certain behavioral patterns, which is related to measures of IQ, social and cognitive maturity, and competence
2. Encoding strategies and personal constructs: units for categorizing events and for self-description
3. Behavior outcome and stimulus outcome expectancies: the degree of success associated with cues or behaviors
4. Subjective stimulus values: motivating and arousing stimuli, reinforcement preferences, aversions
5. Self-regulatory systems and plans: rules and self-regulations for performance and for the organization of complex behavioral sequences

Behavior is also influenced by its consequences or contingencies. Key concepts are positive and negative reinforcement, extinction, and punishment. Like stimuli, reinforcers can originate externally from one's social environment, or internally from one's capacity for self-praise and self-criticism. Positive reinforcement, the adding of something desirable, or negative reinforcement, the deleting of something undesirable, when they occur immediately after a behavior, increase the frequency of that behavior. No reinforcement, or neutral consequences, is termed extinction and is related to decreases in the rate of behavior. Although it is a complicated phenomenon, punishment, an aversive or painful consequence, is usually related to decreases in the rate of behavior.

Drawing on the principle that behavior is influenced by its effects, Mahoney and Thoresen (1974) discussed behavioral change in terms of behavioral designing, which can occur in three ways—establishing a behavior, increasing or maintaining a behavior, and eliminating a behavior. Establishing a behavior can be accomplished through the techniques of shaping, instruction, modeling, and guided participation. Increasing a behavior calls for the addition of positive or negative reinforcers, altering reinforcement schedules, or increasing the frequency of stimuli eliciting certain behaviors. Behaviors can be eliminated by providing no reinforcement (extinction), by decreasing certain stimuli (stimulus control), by punishment, or by reinforcement of incompatible behavioral responses.

The significance of social learning and behaviorally oriented theories for personal adjustment training is that the theories specify the variables the training should concentrate on to change behavior. In the most general sense, adjustment training must focus on both person and environmental variables, because behavior is a function of both. Mischel's (1973) list of person constructs suggests that the target of adjustment training might be any of the following: construction competencies, personal constructs, values, expectations, and self-regulatory systems and plans. The material regarding behavioral designing provides a number of suggestions for utilizing the principles of modeling and reinforcement in accomplishing adjustment training objectives. Whether person and/or environmental personal adjustment approaches are used, we feel that the objectives should be operationally stated, i.e., that the effective behaviors the client will learn be clearly specified in the treatment program.

Detailed descriptions of adjustment strategies following the bebehavioral and social learning emphases are presented in Chapters 6 and 8. The next section of this chapter is devoted to demonstrating that behavior, in this case rehabilitation outcome, is a function of both person and environmental variables. After presenting documentation for that assertion, the chapter concludes with a discussion of the ways in which personal adjustment training can contribute to the resolution of problems in living.

VARIABLES AFFECTING REHABILITATION OUTCOME

Because the theme for adjustment services in rehabilitation is "meeting problems in living," one must begin by identifying the origin of these problems, as Suchman (1965) did in his "rehabilitation as intervening variable model." The variables in Suchman's model depict the elements affecting rehabilitation outcome. First, one must understand the client characteristics (host), cultural characteristics of rehabilitation as a treatment institution (agent), and characteristics of the environment from which rehabilitation clients come and into which they will return. Host, agent, and environment interact with the physical effects of the disability. Rehabilitation services such as personal adjustment training intervene between the interaction of pre-existing conditions and disability and the consequences that would occur without such intervention. Sections to follow elaborate on the interaction of host, agent, environment, and disability variables as they affect rehabilitation outcome. In part, documentation for the influence of a variety of variables on rehabilitation outcome is drawn from a recent annotated bibliography by Rubin and Salley (1973).

Person Variables

Various aspects of person variables are related to reaction to disability and, hence, to rehabilitation outcome.

Organismic Variables   The following generalizations can be made about certain status or organismic characteristics and their relationship to rehabilitation outcome:

1. Age is negatively related to rehabilitation outcome (DeMann, 1963; Neff, Novick, and Stern, 1968; Weiner, 1964).
2. Weiner (1964) found that race was related to rehabilitation outcome, with whites having more positive outcomes.
3. Being married was associated with positive rehabilitation outcomes (Weiner, 1964).
4. Men have been found to have more positive rehabilitation outcomes than women (Neff, Novick, and Stern, 1968).
5. Health is positively related to rehabilitation outcome (McPhee and Magleby, 1960).
6. Being younger at age of onset of disability (DeMann, 1963) and being younger at time of application (Ayer, Thoreson, and Butler, 1966) have both been shown to be related to positive rehabilitation outcome.

Behavioral Competencies   Several studies have found that variables related to behavioral competencies have a significant relationship to rehabilitation outcome:

1. Weiner (1964) found that clients rated average or better on personal adequacy in terms of personal skills had better rehabilitation outcomes.
2. DeMann (1963) and McPhee and Magleby (1960) found that level of educational and vocational training was positively related to rehabilitation outcome.
3. Similarly, higher job skill levels (Weiner, 1964) were also related to rehabilitation outcome.
4. Gilbert and Lester (1970) found that WAIS full scale and performance IQ was related to rehabilitation outcome.

Self-Regulatory Systems and Plans Weiner (1964) found that those clients who actually had vocational plans were more likely to have positive rehabilitation outcomes.

Expectancies Expectations for the treatment program itself can be directly related to the quality of a patient's recovery. For example, Fogel and Rosillo (1969) found that male physically disabled clients who had expectations for what they would achieve in the treatment program tended to make a better recovery. Uncertainties about the future and realizations that one's past expectancies no longer apply to the future have also been related to rehabilitation outcome. For example, Dobson et al. (1971) found that high manifest anxiety scores were associated with poor adjustment to heart attacks. They attributed these high anxiety scores to the uncertainty regarding the future experienced by some clients. Similar findings were reported by Gruen (1975). Shontz (1971) reported that clients must deal with two significant stages—1) realizing that their pre-disability expectations for the future no longer hold, and 2) identifying new expectations for the future. Those clients who are unable to identify positive reasons for living do less well in rehabilitation. Shontz (1971) also quoted research conducted by Lazarus that indicates that the second phase of coping with stress involves estimating the outcomes of different types of coping maneuvers.

Encoding and Personal Constructs MacGuffie (1970) and MacGuffie et al. (1969) found that self-concept was positively related to employment. Linkowski and Dunn (1974) found a positive relationship between self-esteem and acceptance of disability. Use of constructs emphasizing defeat, sickness, and pessimism has been shown to have a negative relationship to rehabilitation outcome (Gilbert and Lester 1970; Gressett, 1969; Shontz, 1971). In analyzing the differential reactions of social security and vocational rehabilitation clients to disability, Cordaro and Shontz (1969) illustrated the importance of encoding. Individuals viewed their disability differently, depending upon whether or not they interpreted the situation to be one that required them to enhance or to diminish the handicapping aspects of their disability. Finally, Colman (1971) discussed the problems that arise when individuals are unable to interpret their situations, e.g., the marginally disabled individual who suffers from a conflict in roles between that of normal and handicapped functioning. Individuals in a more marginal position made a less positive adjustment to disability.

Subjective Stimulus Values   Referring to the things that people find rewarding, the concept of stimulus values also emphasizes the fact that a wide range of individual differences exists regarding what is rewarding. For example, Smith-Hanen (1976) commented on the differences in adjustment to disability that arise out of different reward preferences. She cited one study showing that "lower class females tend to dread facial disfigurement more than middle-class— probably because there are not other methods for self-evaluation, such as artistic or intellectual attainment" (Smith-Hanen, p. 133).

Environmental Variables

The following indicators of the quality of an individual's environment have been related to rehabilitation outcome:

1. Because a stable job history, higher earnings, and educational or vocational training level are related to rehabilitation outcome, it is apparent that environmental opportunities for jobs and training have a bearing on recovery from disability (McPhee and Magleby, 1960; Weiner, 1964).
2. Sivadon and Veil (1968) found that distance of job from home was related to rehabilitation outcome; length of work stoppage increased with distance of job from home.
3. McPhee and Magleby (1960) and Dobson et al. (1971) reported that healthy relationships with the family, particularly the spouse, were related to adjustment to disability.
4. Safilios-Rothschild (1970) discussed how repulsion, fear, and anxiety on the part of the nondisabled are transmitted to the disabled individual. Such feedback from others has a detrimental effect on the disabled individual's self-concept. Furthermore, the nondisabled individual may begin to feel guilty due to unacceptable feelings toward the disabled and display such artificial

behavior as excessive attention and acceptance. Marinelli (1974) found that this anxiety in dealing with the disabled tends to be a problem for the potential rehabilitation professional as well.

5. In a study of rheumatoid arthritis, Wiener (1975) found that the presence of support from the family and economic independence were positively related to the extent to which the individual with arthritis could overcome relapses. Where family support and economic independence were not present, these relapses tended to cause invalidism and social isolation. Dobson (1969) also pointed out the way in which emotional upsets created by others in the family can exacerbate rheumatoid arthritis.

6. Trieschmann (1974) attributed failures in rehabilitation to such environmental aspects as architectural barriers, available medical care, and resources for equipment repair (p. 557).

Smith-Hanen (1976) reviewed several studies that illustrated the way in which one's interpersonal environment can have a detrimental effect on adjustment to disability. Friends and acquaintances find it either difficult to interact with disabled persons, or they actually avoid or abandon them.

Several studies found that parents treat their disabled children as if they were sick, which causes excessive concern with "what is wrong with the child." Parents not only give disabled children more attention, they may also hold them less responsible for their behavior and, in fact, place fewer limits on them. Because they are discrepant with those of other parents, parental expectations for the disabled child interfere with the child's "normal socialization" (Smith-Hanen, 1976, p. 135). Later on, when employment issues emerge, studies show that the support of the family, if it does not escalate into over-support, facilitates employment success (Smith-Hanen, 1976).

Nature of Disability

The relationship of seriousness of disability to rehabilitation outcome is ambiguous. On the one hand, evidence suggests that attitudes of persons toward their own disabilities vary widely and have little relation to the degree of disability (Wright, 1960). On the other hand, rehabilitation outcomes have been shown to be poorer for more encompassing disabilities such as deafness than for reversible disabilities such as pulmonary tuberculosis (DeMann, 1963). Among heart patients, Dobson et al. (1971) found that poorer long-term adjustment was associated with greater physical disability. Colman (1971) found that the more marginal the state of the disabling condition, the more difficulty the person has adjusting to it.

In any case, as Wright (1960) and others have stressed, physical disability does make a profound impact on the individual's life. Serious effects of rheumatoid arthritis include reduction in mobility and skill, constant pain, loss of dexterity, and loss of strength (Wiener, 1975). Shontz (1971) discussed the toxicity-induced psychological symptoms of renal failure. Obviously, the nature of the disability is a significant aspect of the total psychological situation.

Cultural Factors in Rehabilitation

The influence of cultural values on rehabilitation is, in turn, transmitted to disabled individuals. The conflict between the value of "self-help" and charity or support through difficult circumstances is reflected in a number of contradictory practices. For example, Safilios-Rothschild (1970) noted the many conflicting situations presented to the disabled individual by different aspects of the rehabilitation process. For example, Social Security benefits to the disabled emphasize the person's disability, whereas vocational rehabilitation emphasizes the person's ability. Income maintenance available to the disabled worker is often inadequate for the needs of the family, and the worker is forced to withdraw from rehabilitation. Workmen's compensation awards are made on the extent of disability, not on physical injury, and this tends to motivate malingering. Furthermore, the fact that the case can be reopened and re-rated inhibits the worker from trying to make maximal adjustments to the disability. Finally, the extent of time required to establish eligibility and to close the case in rehabilitation services discourages some clients.

After reviewing medical and sociological literature, Safilios-Rothschild (1970) identified several culturally based expectations of physicians, and of other rehabilitation personnel, that can have an impact on client response to disability. From this culturally based point of view of rehabilitation professionals, the rehabilitation client:

1. Should accept his disability and start learning how to "live with it" (p. 74).
2. Should ". . . pull himself together and start carrying on his normal social roles by utilizing to the utmost his capacities and abilities within the restrictions set by the physical impairment" (p. 75).
3. Should, once the disability is stabilized, gear his motivation "toward effective utilization of remaining abilities in order to re-

sume as many of the 'normal' social roles as possible" (p. 76).
4. Should perform "his social roles, tasks, and activities—especially when he is ambulatory" (p. 77).
5. Should "focus upon physical recovery and return to gainful employment rather than live on compensation" (p. 78).

Interaction Position

As indicated previously, ample research evidence exists to suggest that environment, disability, and agent factors independently influence adjustment to disability. The research also strongly suggests that the various factors possess greater explanatory power when combined in a linear equation. It should be emphasized that the term "interaction" is not being used here in its standard statistical sense, i.e., a relationship between two variables that is contingent on a third variable, but is being used to indicate that several variables work together in combination to determine adjustment to disability and rehabilitation outcome. Because the multivariate outcome studies in rehabilitation were recently summarized (see Bolton, 1974b, pp. 180–187), the interested reader is referred to the referenced publication. However, two investigations of hearing-impaired clients that were not included in the review are briefly summarized below to illustrate the "interaction" position.

Bolton (1975) analyzed the relationships of three kinds of client data (biographic, psychometric, and service parameters) to rehabilitation outcome for three samples of deaf clients. The following variables were significantly correlated with employment at follow-up in at least one sample: sex, race, age, schooling, previous work, nonverbal IQ, manual communication, oral-verbal communication, and completion of training. Multiple regression equations that were derived for each of the three client samples accounted for 35%, 23%, and 20% of the variance in employment outcomes.

Interaction of person, environment, agent, and disability factors was the basis for the development of a client feasibility index for hearing-impaired clients (Miller, Kunce, and Getsinger, 1972). The index was based on such variables as age, education, previous number of jobs, previous amount of work time, amount of hearing loss, number of disabilities, race, marital status, number of dependent children, performance IQ, reading grade achievement score, arithmetic grade achievement score, and counselor's recommendation of client employability. Employment, job level, employment persistence, and job stability were also related to the index.

But, what is the importance of showing that these individual factors, separately and collectively, are related to reaction to disability and rehabilitation outcome? According to Suchman (1965), the application of such knowledge should be in the development of rehabilitation strategies. However, some variables, e.g., age, sex, race, marital status, etc., do not lend themselves to change. Hence, adjustment strategies must be based on aspects of person, environment, disability, and agent that can be modified. Because this book is concerned with psychosocial adjustment, the emphasis in subsequent chapters is on ways to enhance the disabled individual's psychological abilities to cope with problems in living created by the physical/medical and personal/social aspects of disability.

RESOLVING PROBLEMS IN LIVING
THROUGH PERSONAL ADJUSTMENT TRAINING

Because they are somewhat outside of the realm of personal adjustment training, many of the medical and environmental responses that can be made to help individuals adjust to disability are not covered in detail in this book. The focus is on the variety of personal adjustment training strategies that have been designed to facilitate clients' personal development and adjustment to disability. Concentrating on aspects of human behavior that can be changed, these adjustment strategies reflect the experience and research of several individuals (Anthony, Margoles, and Collingwood, 1974; Bolton, 1976; Gordon, 1971; Roessler, 1972).

One useful way to categorize the variety of available adjustment services is in the context of the levels of rehabilitation outcome that Trieschmann (1974) defined as appropriate rehabilitation expectations for the severely disabled. In order to move away from a universal goal of employment, she proposed a sliding scale of goals responsive to the unique physical and environmental circumstances of severely disabled clients. Although coping with disability is still the hallmark of rehabilitation, Trieschmann's system allows for different levels of proficiency in resolving the problems in living related to disability.

The three aspects of outcome include: 1) prevention of medical complications and utilization of Activities of Daily Living (ADL) mobility skills, 2) maintenance of a stable living environment, and 3) productivity. The flexibility in rehabilitation outcome is introduced in the sense that aspects of each category may apply "to each disabled individual depending upon age, level of function, environment and behavioral style" (Trieschmann, 1974, p. 557). In other words, the rehabilitation plan for a client may emphasize goals at one, two, or all three of the levels.

The first level, prevention of medical complication and utilization of ADL-mobility skills, requires that the person demonstrate self-care ability or the ability to secure necessary health care from the environment. Personal adjustment services in this area would include many of the skills provided through physical therapy, occupational therapy, mobility training, and activities of daily living training emphasizing self-care.

Maintenance of a stable living environment, the second level, includes maintaining a residence, meeting physical needs, and coping with family and social factors. Adjustment training at this level should emphasize the development of personal skills. For example, Gordon (1971) defined socialization skills as including the following: 1) the ability to size up social situations and to act appropriately, 2) the ability to read expectations of a group, 3) the ability to relate to others, and 4) the ability to exercise personal control over one's life.

In an article focusing on personal skill development, Roessler (1972) specified several problem areas that can be responded to directly through some type of adjustment training:

1. Problem: inability to interact satisfactorily with others
   Training: interpersonal skills
2. Problem: ineffective behaviors in important life situations
   Training: life skills modeling
3. Problem: low achievement need and drive
   Training: achievement motivation training
4. Problem: expectation of little control over one's fate
   Training: internal control training
5. Problem: minimal desire to set personal goals and to devise ways to achieve those goals
   Training: capacity for self-direction training
6. Problem: poor physical fitness
   Training: physical fitness training

Anthony, Margoles, and Collingwood (1974) added other skills that clients could learn in order to maintain a stable living environment. For example, clients need problem solving skills, community living skills (use of transportation, recreational facilities, etc.), and emotional and interpersonal skills. Bolton (1976) noted the need among multiply handicapped deaf clients for communications training, marriage and family living skills, avocational counseling, consumer services, and citizenship. Of course, the adjustment needs cited by Bolton—marriage and family living skills, sexual counseling, and consumer services—exist for many other disability groups as well.

Trieschmann's (1974) third and final level, productivity, includes vocational, educational, social, and avocational outcomes. To meet aspects of the productive level, the person is involved in some concrete way in work, school, volunteer services, or personal hobbies. Training strategies that fit the productivity emphasis include a variety of educational, vocational, and/or avocational services. For example, clients must upgrade many of their technical skills (Gordon, 1971) such as reading, writing, oral communication, and computation. Anthony, Margoles, and Collingwood (1974) emphasized career development skills, job interviewing skills, and such intellectual skills as money management, job seeking, and job application skills.

Overall, the personal skills development approach to the three levels of rehabilitation outcome is aimed at helping clients learn to respond in more effective ways to problems in living. Of course, one should not exclude the many environmental changes that would enhance an individual's adjustment to disability. For example, the availability of educational and vocational training settings is important, as are accessibility to medical services, equipment repair, public and private facilities, and work settings. Available jobs with adequate wages are needed. Attitudes of the nondisabled toward the disabled require modification, as do the attitudes, often, of family and friends. However, as noted in Chapter 1, attitudes toward disability are highly resistant to change.

Many factors in the institution of rehabilitation itself can be changed to provide greater support to the disabled. Counselors can learn what their expectations and projections regarding the disabled are, and how these affect counseling outcomes. Also, current efforts to democratize the rehabilitation process, e.g., the individualized written rehabilitation program, will help clients accomplish goals of personal importance.

Counterincentives, such as Social Security's emphasis on disability and Vocational Rehabilitation's stress on ability, should be examined and lessened. Workmen's compensation might be defined to compensate extent of injury and not disability, so that individuals would not be rewarded for exaggerating loss of functioning. Similarly, a one-time settlement of the case would not cause individuals to fear that later rehabilitation gains might lead to a decrease in compensation. Rapid eligibility determination and sufficient living support are also needed (Safilios-Rothschild, 1970).

SUMMARY

The purpose of adjustment services is to help clients cope with life demands. Because of the heterogeneity of life demands, personal adjustment training includes a wide variety of different client services. One rationale for personal adjustment training focuses on the behavioral and social learning orientations. The basic emphasis is on helping clients develop the effective behaviors they need to cope with a succession of situations. The behavioral or social learning orientation emphasizes several key notions of adjustment, such as the need for observable criteria, the concept of cultural relativity, and the importance of individual uniqueness. A key principle for adjustment services is that behavior is a function of the interaction of person and environment. To change behavior, one must concentrate on the modification of such person variables as construction competencies, personal constructs, expectations, values, and plans. The role of the environment in behavioral change must also be acknowledged. For example, the principles of vicarious learning and reinforcement can be used in the development of effective adjustment strategies. The desirable direction of change is to enable the individual to develop the coping skills needed to deal more effectively with problems in living. Resolving problems in living for the disabled can occur on at least three levels—prevention of medical complications and utilization of daily living skills, maintenance of a stable living environment, and productivity.

Chapter 4

Severe Disability:
Spinal Cord Injury

The Rehabilitation Act of 1973 mandated that the "most severely disabled" receive priority in vocational rehabilitation. While there is no current definition of "most severely disabled," one type of physical impairment, spinal cord injury, clearly meets the criteria and legislative intent of a severe disability. Given the fact that spinal cord injury has profound physiological, economic, and psychosocial effects, it follows that rehabilitation must be comprehensive in scope.

In order to expand and intensify services for the spinal cord injured, an experimental treatment project was initiated in 1975 by the Arkansas Rehabilitation Services at the Central Baptist Hospital in Little Rock, and the Hot Springs Rehabilitation Center, Hot Springs, Arkansas. The Spinal Cord Injury Project integrated intermediate hospital care, personal and vocational evaluation and training, individual, group, sexual, and family counseling services, physical and occupational therapy, and follow-along services. Additional services in the home and community were provided by the Project's field personnel.

The material in this chapter provides an overview of the Arkansas Spinal Cord Injury Project and of the psychosocial adjustment ramifications of a severe disability like spinal cord injury. Consistent with the personal adjustment training thrust of this book, special attention is given in the final section to implementation of Personal Achievement Skills Training (a package that is described in detail in Chapter 6) with spinal cord injured clients.

SERVING THE SPINAL CORD INJURED

Spinal cord injury (SCI), a catastrophic impairment placing severe functional limitations on an individual, is so physically debilitating that until recently few persons survived the trauma of injury. With significant medical advances and the consequent increase in the survival rate of the spinal cord injured, medical management and the psychosocial problems related to spinal cord damage have become salient concerns in current research. To illustrate, of more than 3,000 spinal cord injury studies published between 1940 and 1963, only 70 articles were concerned with psychosocial adjustment to SCI and to the related psychosocial problems (Little and Stewart, 1975). By July of 1976, approximately 700 studies addressing psychological adjustment, vocational outcomes, and environmental functioning of the spinal cord injured were available in the literature.

Physical needs of the spinal cord injured have been reviewed elsewhere in the literature in considerable detail. For example, Bors (1956) and O'Connor and Leitner (1971) discussed such physical complications of spinal cord injury as spinal shock, spasticity, management of elimination, decubiti, and cardiac and pulmonary complications. Therefore, ensuing sections of this chapter concentrate on the psychosocial aspects of spinal cord injury.

Review of Psychosocial Research

Four out of five spinal cord injured persons are male, most of whom are young (15 to 30 years of age) and have a pre-injury history of activity. Auto accidents are the number one cause of spinal cord injuries, followed by gunshot wounds, diving, and falling accidents. Paraplegia is the most common result of spinal cord injury. Currently there are approximately 125,000 spinal cord injured in the United States, with approximately 6,000 to 10,000 newly injured persons each year. On a national level, the Rehabilitation Services Administration (RSA) estimates 20% of the total national spinal cord injured population to be potential consumers of rehabilitation services.

In an extensive literature review, Cook (1976) pointed out that researchers and clinicians in the field are in general agreement that it is a person's premorbid personality that determines how that person will react to spinal cord injury. Even though every spinal cord injured person is likely to exhibit an idiosyncratic adjustment pattern, all newly injured persons are faced with the problem of extreme physical and psychological dependency.

Other research has suggested that there may be different psychological types among the spinal cord injured. For example, Fordyce (1964) isolated two groups of spinal cord injured males. One group was younger, impulse-dominated, and tended to have been injured in imprudent or high risk types of accidents. The other group was older, prudent, and tended to have been injured in chance accidents. Presumably the first group might be more susceptible to behavioral problems amenable to psychosocial treatment.

Cook's (1976) review pointed out that considerable research interest has been directed at the role of depression in adjustment to spinal cord injury. Early clinical research suggested that depression was a normal and expected reaction to the impairment. Some authors (e.g., Siller, 1969) have included depression in a theory of adjustment to spinal cord injury, linking it with the concept of mourning. Empirical research has, however, questioned whether or not depression or mourning over loss is a necessary precondition in the adjustment process. In fact, some studies have suggested that spinal cord transection may physiologically modify a spinal cord injured person's emotional responses. Other studies suggest that the spinal cord injured may be learning, from implied staff attitudes, that they are required to enter a period of mourning or suffer periods of depression.

Little and Stewart (1975) and Poor (1975) have completed literature reviews in which they outlined some of the key variables thought to relate to successful rehabilitation outcome. Considering vocational self-sufficiency as a higher-order type of rehabilitation outcome, one of the key considerations is functional limitations associated with the impairment. The degree of physical limitation is, of course, important in determining realistic vocational goals. Because of the nature of spinal cord injury and associated medical complications, career development and vocational placement may also be limited by environmental constraints, architectural barriers, limitations in transportation systems, and prejudice of the able-bodied.

As in the disabled population in general, age, educational level, and work history are related to vocational outcomes for the spinal cord injured. A favorable premorbid work history, younger age, and higher educational level are indicators of more successful vocational outcomes. Family support and the kind and degree of community resources are other factors influencing rehabilitation outcomes. Kemp and Vash (1971) found, when outcome was recast in terms of productivity (indexed as employment, community activity, independent living, etc.), that the key factor in separating productive from nonproductive spinal cord injured was that the more productive persons had, during rehabilitation, expressed a larger number of goals.

Finally, it should be noted that not all of the spinal cord injured have vocational potential. For example, Dinsdale, Lesser, and Judd (1971) studied a sample of spinal cord injured and were able to differentiate three distinct subgroups. One group was mainly concerned with independence training and return to a central family role; another group was concerned with regaining lost functions and vocational retraining; and the third group had few goals and a marginal prognosis. Considering the multitude of barriers facing the spinal cord injured and the differences in individual goals (e.g., physical restoration vs. vocational retraining), it may be best to expect different kinds of successful outcome based on individual levels of functional limitations.

In addition, the fact that spinal cord injured persons face multiple barriers is all the more reason for a comprehensive service response. Abramson (1967) has discussed the need for holistic, comprehensive, and flexible approaches for the spinal cord injured, stressing that this concept of treatment was, unfortunately, a viewpoint and not an actuality. According to Abramson, neither the knowledge of the "biology of paraplegia" nor of the "sociologic and psychologic principles" involved have been integrated into rehabilitation of the spinal cord injured. Although Abramson's observations apply for the most part, efforts have been made recently to provide coordinated and inclusive services to the spinal cord injured.

Comprehensive Service Programs

According to the Report of the Comprehensive Needs Study (McNickle, 1975), the first comprehensive treatment facility for the spinal cord injured was established in 1944 at Stoke-Mandeville Hospital in England. Similar centralized treatment facilities were soon developed in Australia and Poland. In the United States, the development of comprehensive, regional spinal cord treatment centers was spearheaded by the Veteran's Administration (VA). In fact, much of the knowledge on the care and restoration of the spinal cord injured is a direct result of pioneering research conducted by the VA. The concept of regional centers to provide centralized comprehensive care for the civilian spinal cord injured is at present a high priority for the Rehabilitation Services Administration. Currently, there are ten such "model centers" in operation throughout the country.

Besides the humanistic concern for reducing the effects of impairment, the regional center concept is seen as a method for reducing the astronomical cost associated with spinal cord injury. For example, lifetime costs average $325,000 to $400,000 for a quadriplegic and $180,000 to $225,000 for a paraplegic. The National Institute for Neurological Disease and Stroke estimated the annual cost of the impairment, nationwide, at $2.4 billion (McNickle, 1975, p. 473). Research conducted at Good Samaritan Hospital in Phoenix, Arizona, the first of the RSA-supported regional centers, has resulted in "reduced costs of initial hospitalization and rehabilitation from more than $30,000 to approximately $11,000. Also yearly follow-up care has been reduced from $3,000 to $500 per patient" (RSA, 1976, p. 66).

A regional service delivery system has been described as follows:

> In an effective system of spinal cord injury treatment and rehabilitation, the person who breaks his back or neck is immediately transported by trained emergency personnel to the spinal cord injury center. From the original surgery through discharge and follow-along services, the key element is the team of specialists. Just as the neurosurgeon needs considerable expertise in the early stage, so do the other specialist involved in the prevention of bladder infections, pressure sores, bowel complications, contractures, and psychological problems. Effective rehabilitation nursing and physical, occupational, and recreational therapy help the paraplegic maximize his independence in activities of daily living. (McNickle, 1975, pp. 472–473)

The concept of interrelated regional treatment centers is a necessary approach to service delivery. For example, Spangler (1966) surveyed spinal cord injured in three states regarding their rehabilitation needs. Of those responding, few had received treatment through a comprehensive rehabilitation center. All persons surveyed expressed a need for comprehensive treatment. Services received were usually through general hospitals, all of which lacked the specially trained personnel required to care for the spinal cord injured. Of course, the most effective service delivery system not only utilizes specialized personnel, but is also systematic, in that acute, long-term, and follow-up care are coordinated. In 1975, the Arkansas Rehabilitation Services implemented a program coupling hospital, rehabilitation center, and follow-up services to provide more effective services to the spinal cord injured in Arkansas.

An Exemplary Project

With funding and support from the Rehabilitation Services Administration, the Arkansas Rehabilitation Services developed a "model" Spinal Cord Rehabilitation Project. The Project focused on a number of different objectives, ranging from case finding to follow-up concerns. The initial objective stressed establishment of an outreach system for identifying and referring spinal cord injured clients. Various steps were necessary to accomplish this objective, including:

1. Strategic statewide assignment of Project staff
2. Identification of referral sources
3. Informing referral sources of the Project
4. Referral procurement
5. Maintenance of a spinal cord injured registry in Arkansas

Another objective involved developing individual rehabilitation plans with clients that stressed long-term comprehensive training for both individuals with spinal cord injuries and their families. These rehabilitation plans also called for use of the multiple services of the Hot Springs Rehabilitation Center, as well as later attention to continuity of services in follow-up care. In the initial phases of the client's plan, other agencies and organizations were to be included to provide rapid evaluation and transportation, immediate medical services, and intermediate medical services.

The Project also required program evaluation and research activities. Project evaluation data were collected, not only to provide an estimate of Project effectiveness, but also to suggest ways to improve Project services. The next section describes in more detail the Project's services and staffing.

Project Staffing Patterns

The Project followed the philosophy of providing centralized and systematic treatment to the spinal cord injured from the moment of injury through community reentry. The strategy adopted identified those to be served, provided increased resources through the assignment of specialized staff, utilized specialized staff to provide linkages between acute and long-term treatment, adopted comprehensive rehabilitation services to meet the specialized needs of the spinal cord injured, and measured the impact of the program. The direct service component of the program consisted of assigning staff to positions in the field at an intermediate care facility, and at a comprehensive rehabilitation center.

A project director, one full-time counselor, two half-time counselors, one social worker, a physical therapist, an occupational therapist, a nurse, and two clerical persons were assigned to the Hot Springs Rehabilitation Center. Two counselors, a placement counselor, a social worker, and two clerical persons were assigned to the intermediate facility, Central Baptist Hospital. Finally, three full-time and two half-time rehabilitation counselors provided service to spinal cord injured persons in their respective regions throughout the state. Field counselors obtained referrals in their area and held cases in referral status until completion of medical evaluation and an appropriate rehabilitation plan. During acute and intermediate care, field counselors had the responsibility to provide counseling, maintain family communication, and, generally, monitor client progress. Persons who entered either Central Baptist Hospital or the Hot Springs Rehabilitation Center received case services from Project staff at those institutions.

Several changes in the staffing patterns took place during the program. In August of 1976, the job placement position was deleted from the Project. Also, the Project became associated with the Arkansas Spinal Cord Commission, a statewide commission charged with examining the plight of the spinal cord injured in Arkansas. Through an agreement between the Commission and the Arkansas Rehabilitation Services, six extra rehabilitation counselors assumed regional spinal cord injured case responsibilities. In addition to expanding in-the-field coverage of spinal cord injured persons eligible for vocational rehabilitation, all ten counselors assumed coordinating responsibilities for other spinal cord injured cases, mainly children with spina bifida.

Project Services

Because the spinal cord injured have multiple needs, the Project aimed at providing a full regimen of needed services at the appropriate time. For example, the first consideration of any spinal cord injury service program is the survival of the injured person. Accordingly, evacuation, transportation, and immediate medical treatment is a prime consideration. Project resources included a statewide Emergency Medical Service System for immediate evacuation and transportation, with communication channels to involve appropriate agencies in evacuation of the newly spinal cord injured. Immediate medical services, available at the hospital nearest the site of injury, included such emergency treatment as surgery, medication, and nursing care. Project staff could not, at this stage of treatment, offer financial resources for all spinal cord injured persons. They were able, however, to explain services available through vocational rehabilitation and to assist in obtaining financial support through other sources.

Once the person was medically stabilized to the extent that the injury was no longer acutely life-threatening, he/she entered the intermediate care facility. At this point, Project personnel played a progressively greater role, monitoring the progress of the person, explaining services available, and assisting in treatment planning. Through joint planning with associate staff, psychosocial adjustment strategies and preliminary assessments of the person's vocational potential were developed.

After the client was accepted for vocational rehabilitation and entered either extended evaluation or training, Project personnel became even more involved. While extended evaluation could be conducted at either the intermediate facility, Central Baptist Hospital, or the Hot Springs Rehabilitation Center, the intent of the system was to enroll the spinal cord injured in the Center program. Services offered by the Center included: medical treatment, counseling, vocational evaluation and training, physical and occupational therapy, orthotics, and adult driver education training, as well as social and psychological consultation.

Because of the gravity of the disability, the Project provided for expanded and intensified services to spinal cord injured enrolled at the Hot Springs Rehabilitation Center. For example, the Project assigned two on-site counselors to work specifically with spinal cord injured persons enrolled at the Center. Other treatment innovations included an in-depth client orientation to the ramifications of spinal cord impairment, establishment of a pre-discharge program to facilitate community readjustment, and the provision of specialized leisure-recreational programs.

Finally, the Project was designed to assist the spinal cord injured's reentry into the community. Project personnel were to ensure a continuity of care through an organized long-term follow-up program that attended to community adjustment. Results regarding the impact of Project services are discussed in the next section.

RESEARCH REVIEW

The initial evaluation report for the Spinal Cord Injured Project (Cook and Roessler, 1977) provides a psychological profile of spinal cord injured clients and a preliminary assessment of Project effectiveness. Data on 172 vocational rehabilitation clients were collected either at the Central Baptist Hospital (the intermediate care facility) or at the Hot Springs Rehabilitation Center. Of the total group of 172 referrals, 57 completed the psychological battery. Demographic, medical, vocational, and economic characteristics for this subsample are essentially identical to those of the total group.

Results

Results of the demographic analysis, psychological profile, and preliminary program evaluation are summarized as follows:

1. The ratio of individuals suffering paraplegia to those suffering quadriplegia was two to one in the sample. Basic primary medical complications of spinal cord injury included urological (32%), respiratory (25%), and dermatological (22%) problems. Postdisability income was largely derived from sources other than wages, i.e., Social Security Disability Insurance, parents, and/or spouse.

2. Clients for whom psychological data were available tended to stress independence-related goals for their rehabilitation program, e.g., getting a driver's license (14%), getting and holding a job (16%), and being more independent (18%).

3. Deviating from patterns of the normative population and those of a general disabled group, life ladder ratings of these spinal cord injured clients were U-shaped, i.e., past and future were rated higher than present.

4. Spinal cord injured clients compared favorably with a disabled norm group on need satisfaction in the areas of emotional security and family life. However, they reported higher need satisfaction than the comparison disabled group on social, economic security, economic self-esteem, vocational self-actualization, and total scale scores.

5. Mini-Mult (a brief version of the Minnesota Multiphasic Personality Inventory) scale scores suggested that, on the average, these spinal cord injured clients did not evidence severe psychological maladjustment. Surprisingly, clients reported state and trait anxiety levels somewhat lower than those of general medical-surgical clients, and very similar to those of a normative sample of college students.

6. One method for estimating Project effectiveness required an analysis of the Project's penetration into the population of spinal cord injured persons in the state. Based on projections of the number of SCI clients, the program contacted a higher than expected number of SCI clients for rehabilitation services.

7. Another Project objective had to do with establishing linkages

with other agencies, which included providing clients with transportation. Fewer arrangements for transportation were made than might be expected.

8. Carrying caseloads of 16 clients per month, counselors averaged 30 client contacts a month, with substantial variation among counselors. Contacts focused primarily on discussing services, vocational concerns, and personal adjustment.

9. Of those clients who were subsequently enrolled at the Hot Springs Rehabilitation Center (HSRC), about half saw the primary reasons for their stay to be medical evaluation or surgical treatment. Vocational training was the perceived primary purpose for only a quarter of these clients. Although using general medicine and physical therapy services, clients at HSRC seemed to underutilize vocational services such as work evaluation, vocational training, and job placement.

10. Center counselors had extensive contact with SCI clients that focused basically on coordination of services, coping skills, and client sexual concerns. Social workers also stayed in close contact with clients, with most of their effort being devoted to service coordination between field and Center counselors.

Implications

Based on results summarized above, the following conclusions and/or broad implications were derived:

1. Clients injured at or before age 18 (41% of those in the Project) have been in a dependent status for a significant period of time. Having developed few vocational commitments and behaviors, these clients present a considerable challenge to the vocational rehabilitation counselor. Complicating vocational counseling was the fact that many clients had, before their injury, only subsistence incomes, which could be equaled by postdisability financial support from family and other sources.

2. Most SCI clients viewed rehabilitation as access to medical and surgical services. Possibly, these clients felt that rehabilitation does not provide adequate vocational services for the spinal cord injured. On the other hand, clients may not have developed enough security regarding their medical condition to consider vocations seriously. Clients might have lacked a clear understanding of the vocational and psychological services available through a comprehensive center; hence, a client orientation program would be beneficial.

3. Diversity of goals selected by SCI clients underscores the need for individualized planning with clients; a "preplanned" series of services for all clients would seem to be less effective than more individualized services. Independence goals are somewhat more important to clients than vocational or social goals. Possibly, accomplishments in independent living skills would pave the way to working on vocational and social goals.

4. Like other disabled client groups, Project clients reported low satisfaction levels of work, psychological, and health-related needs. To meet the needs of spinal cord injured clients more effectively, several steps must be taken. First, the crucial problems in these need areas must be identified and resolved. Vocational training programs must be modified to meet the physical limitations of the spinal cord injured. Development of additional vocational alternatives must also be continued.

5. Direct counseling with clients regarding their goals and objectives for the future is also required. The counselor should focus on whether the client holds a realistic perspective or one that is excessively hopeful, to the point of denying obvious implications of the injury.

6. Psychological adjustment to spinal cord injury is highly idiosyncratic. For example, only one-fifth of the sample expressed any depressive reaction, which is often presumed to be related to spinal cord injury. Little deleterious anxiety was evident in the group. Therefore, counselors should be aware of the dangers of overgeneralizations regarding the psychological impact of spinal cord injury.

7. Project procedures for identifying and involving spinal cord injured individuals in rehabilitation services appeared effective. However, examination of the reasons for the Project's deviation from the expected progression of services for a number of clients is needed. For example, only six percent of the vocational rehabilitation referred group followed the expected treatment progression of referral, intermediate care, and comprehensive rehabilitation.

The Spinal Cord Injury Project also had many significant implications for personal adjustment training. These implications are discussed in the concluding section of this chapter.

PERSONAL ADJUSTMENT TRAINING
WITH SPINAL CORD INJURED CLIENTS

At the inception of the Spinal Cord Injury Project, it was recognized that supplementary services in the personal adjustment area would be needed. In particular, individuals associated with the design of the Project and the delivery of services felt a need to involve clients with spinal cord injuries in a group counseling setting. Group counseling should emphasize the development of basic skills, such as interpersonal skills and problem solving skills, and the opportunity for clients to participate in developing their own rehabilitation plans. Hence, an experimental Personal Achievement Skills group was started at the Hot Springs Rehabilitation Center.

Conducting an evaluation of the Personal Achievement Skills program proved to be more difficult than was anticipated. In fact, more was learned about the difficulties of providing personal adjustment services than about the actual impact of the program. Significant points pertinent to the delivery of adjustment services and to the additional adjustment services required by individuals with spinal cord injuries were summarized in a recent article (Roessler, Milligan, and Ohlson, 1976).

Personal Achievement Skills[1]

As part of their comprehensive treatment program, five paraplegics and five quadriplegics participated in Personal Achievement Skills Training (PAS). Because PAS focuses on personal functioning, goal identification, and goal achievement within a group setting, the program can contribute to realism and clarity in aspirations and to the identification of possible alternatives for one's life, both of which have been related to adjustment to paralysis (Kemp and Wetmore 1969–1970; Rabinowitz, 1961).

Ten clients in the Spinal Cord Injury Project were randomly assigned to PAS and ten to a control group. Self-report measures of psychological adjustment were administered at the beginning of the program and scheduled for readministration at the end. However, the program evaluation was never completed due to the high rate of attrition in both the experimental and control groups (60 and 80%, respectively). Despite the incomplete nature of the experimental study, the personal adjustment staff gained a deeper insight into the PAS program itself, into the problems in conducting personal adjustment training with the spinal cord injured, and into the

---

[1]This section is adapted from Roessler, Milligan, and Ohlson (1976), with permission of the copyright holder, the American Personnel and Guidance Association.

needs of spinal cord injured clients in a comprehensive rehabilitation program.

For example, the two students who regularly attended PAS achieved significant goals and improved in rated current adjustment. Each of the participants wrote and completed a goal program. One 20-year-old male, impaired since age 15, developed an independent living goal that included the following phases: 1) find out what I need to do to prepare myself physically, 2) learn the skills I will need to live on my own, 3) practice budgeting and banking, 4) develop friendships away from the Center, and 5) move from the Center and live independently.

Each phase was broken down into specific behavioral steps. For example, in the first phase (find out what I need to do to prepare myself physically), the client listed three steps: 1) talk with four other paraplegics now living independently, 2) talk with physical therapists at the Center to find out if they think I am physically ready, and 3) complete any physical therapy necessary to become physically ready.

Participation in PAS may have only been the catalyst for this client to act on a strong drive toward independence, but that in itself is important for the spinal cord injured. The client registered other changes. He became active in an effort to establish independent living training as part of the regular Center curriculum. His counselor noted a marked drop in minor disciplinary problems and reported that the client was currently living independently in the community.

The other client, injured at age 20, was 23 when he participated in PAS. He had a history of disdaining "school-type" activities, but later realized that he needed to make specific plans for his future. His goal program was a comprehensive one, including the following seven phases: 1) identify available jobs that pay adequately, 2) obtain General Education Diploma (GED) certificate, 3) obtain driver's license, 4) enroll in data processing, 5) improve study habits, 6) develop independent living skills, and 7) get a job.

The client received his driver's license and is now enrolled in the GED program and in data processing training. He is also preparing to move into the community.

Although only two clients actually completed the goal-setting phase of the program, eight of the ten involved students requested further group counseling. Those working with the clients in the group session felt that PAS stimulated a need in the clients to share experiences in a meaningful way.

Admittedly, the minimal results regarding the PAS program pertain only to those who completed the program. Furthermore, the goal programs of the two individuals who completed the program may say more about the individuals themselves or about their situation than about the effectiveness of PAS. However, observed changes in personal adjustment and the achievement of significant goals in realistic ways reflect an important outcome for these individuals. Another important outcome of the overall program pertained to the many implications for personal adjustment training that resulted. Such implications ranged from comments about attendance to guidelines for PAS training itself.

Attendance Poor attendance diminishes the impact of any personal adjustment program, particularly one such as PAS, which builds on sequential experiences. Participants in the program missed a number of sessions, mainly for medical reasons. Clients should be screened to ensure that they are medically able to participate in the program.

Student attendance in personal adjustment training also depends on staff commitment to get students to the program on time. The staff must understand the role of personal adjustment training and be convinced of its merit. Attendance is also affected by outside issues, such as family pressures to return home and other family problems. These family problems could be mediated by staff members until the clients complete their facility program.

Attrition Rate Dropping out of PAS occurred when students completed other Center programs, such as physical therapy or occupational therapy, and left for home. In several cases, these students had not completed the PAS program, which required at least six weeks of participation. Again, involvement in personal adjustment training requires facility-wide commitment to it as an integral treatment element.

Group Cohesion In any group counseling program, the importance of group cohesion cannot be minimized. Barriers to group cohesion for spinal cord injured clients occur at both psychological and physical levels. The group leader can at least eliminate physical barriers to cohesion early in the group by moving clients from wheelchairs onto comfortable chairs or couches, where clients would not have to be overly concerned about what would happen if, for example, a leg bag should break. It is important to keep the wheelchairs convenient to the group training area and to have equipment nearby for problems such as leg bag breaks. Naturally, moving clients from wheelchairs requires someone trained in transferring individuals with different types of spinal cord injuries.

Group Composition   In the PAS groups, homogeneity can be a problem. All participants of this group were males and of approximately the same age. Group leaders felt that females could have contributed considerably to the group, particularly in the discussions of problems of sexuality. There is also a need for individuals of varied ages, with varying lengths of disability, who could provide insights into the adjustment problems ahead. Heterogeneity regarding age, sex, length of disability, and type of adjustment would provide enriched feedback for group members.

Leader Participation   The leader needs to have: 1) leadership abilities in group counseling programs, 2) knowledge of spinal cord injury (e.g., of the effects of different levels of injury), and 3) the ability to recognize and deal with emergency medical situations. Medical assistance should be sought immediately when the leader sees such symptoms as sweating, dizziness, slurred speech, loss of facial color, fainting, and so on.

Screening Interview   At least one screening interview is suggested for discussing purposes and expectations of the group. In the screening interview, the leader can determine the client's interest in a group counseling experience that focuses on communication and goal-setting skills. Clients must be ready to take a realistic look at their capacities and desires so that they can begin to make concrete plans for the future. The screening interview might also determine whether or not there are any outstanding problems, such as family difficulties, that would make the client's participation unfeasible at the current time.

Program Demands   PAS requires a minimum IQ of 70 to 80 and the ability to read and write. Writing can be a real problem, particularly for quadriplegics. Quadriplegics might tape record their responses to exercises and have these tapes transcribed at the end of the session. Of course, the participants must be assured of confidentiality.

Length of Session   Since the recommended length of a PAS session is two to two and one-half hours, the fatigue factor for spinal cord injured clients must be considered. Sessions need to be scheduled after either a morning break or lunch. Schedule conflicts, such as those with medical services, must be considered in determining session times.

Other Needs of the Spinal Cord Injured

Implementing recommendations for improving personal adjustment training for the spinal cord injured can make a significant contribution to the effectiveness of the training. In addition, other psychosocial needs of spinal cord injured clients appeared during the course of the Project; they are discussed in the following paragraphs.

Orientation   An orientation program for newly admitted spinal cord injured patients might feature a videotape of an individual with a spinal cord injury relating experiences in adjusting to the handicap and in completing a rehabilitation program. The taped presentation might be followed by a group discussion led by a trained leader. Another feature of the orientation program might be a self-help peer counseling approach, in which new clients receive orientation and support from clients who have been at the facility for a longer period of time.

Family Counseling   Family counseling should begin the very first day that the client enters the facility. Immediate family members will need information about the individual's medical needs, some insight into how to communicate effectively, and orientation as to how they can help the individual deal with his or her disability. Clients and their spouses also need sexual counseling and training. Facility staff need to recognize that family counseling is not a "one-shot" contact but rather requires continual attention to the client and the family throughout the rehabilitation process.

Sequence of Counseling Experiences   The effect of a sequence of counseling experiences might be investigated with the spinal cord injured. The initial experience might be one of involving PAS with a group that is homogeneous as to disability. The homogeneity of the group might allow participants to establish a sense of common bond and group identity. After completion of PAS, participants might move to a group counseling experience involving individuals with a variety of disabilities. The mixed group experience would enable individuals with spinal cord injury to deal with attitudes toward themselves, attitudes toward others, and perceived reactions of others. It is essential that individuals preparing to depart from the Center work with an individual counselor on applying the techniques of goal setting to life situations beyond the facility.

Independent Living Training   Clients obviously need instruction in the area of independent living, which involves such problems as judging an apartment's suitability, budgeting, home safety, self-care, community resources, architectural barriers, driver's training, and the like.

Vocational Training Opportunities   There is a desperate need for additional vocational opportunities for the spinal cord injured. In many cases, identifying appropriate vocational opportunities may require facility personnel to visit work sites in order to investigate jobs that may be suitable for the spinal cord injured. Personnel might then return to the facility and modify existing training programs to prepare the client for such jobs. Vocational training should: 1) establish on-the-job training as much as possible, and 2) try to return the individual to an occupation similar to the preinjury type of work.

Recreation and Leisure Time Training Clients need help in identifying satisfying and creative ways to use the periods during the day when they are not working or sleeping. Developing habits of creative use of leisure time requires reinforcement of participation in facility activities as well as assistance to the individual who has left the facility.

Physical Fitness Training Staff members also noted that several clients requested access to physical fitness equipment in the evenings in order to include additional physical conditioning in their recreational programs. Such clients might profit from the systematic physical fitness program described in Chapter 7, which is currently being adapted for the spinal cord injured by Milligan and Roessler (1977).

SUMMARY

Spinal cord injury is a severely incapacitating disability that requires comprehensive rehabilitation services. Extensive research on the psychosocial and vocational aspects of adjustment to SCI during the past decade has extended the knowledge base for the provision of services. A comprehensive rehabilitation program for SCI clients includes three phases: immediate medical treatment in a hospital; intermediate treatment in a rehabilitation facility, emphasizing psychosocial adjustment and vocational planning; and a long-term follow-up component that focuses on reentry into the community. The preliminary results of the Arkansas SCI Project have numerous implications for service delivery, e.g., individual planning is a necessity with this population, vocational training programs may require substantial modification with SCI clients, psychological adjustment to SCI is highly idiosyncratic, etc. An experimental study of a systematic personal adjustment training program with SCI clients resulted in a number of pertinent considerations, e.g., heterogeneous group composition is desirable, special leader qualifications are necessary, etc. Several other components of a comprehensive program for SCI clients are recommended: special orientation, family counseling, independent living training, recreation and leisure time training, and physical fitness training.

Chapter 5

Adjustment Training in Rehabilitation Services

To develop a foundation for personal adjustment training, a social learning/behavioral model of human behavior is presented in Chapter 3. The person/environment interaction emphasis in the model implies that personal adjustment services must help individuals develop new skills in order to cope with environmental demands. The skill approach to personal adjustment training is consistent with the process orientation to adjustment discussed in Chapter 1, i.e., individuals must learn how to adjust on a situation-by-situation basis.

Because human reaction to disability is an extremely complex issue, personal adjustment training programs must emanate from an individualized diagnosis of needs and skill deficits. In addition, because the emphasis is on helping clients meet a variety of environmental demands, adjustment training must be responsive to the subculture or subcultures in which the client is acting. Hence, a heterogeneous approach is taken in personal adjustment training, in that clients may need to learn behaviors and responses that allow them to operate effectively in different subcultures.

Stressing coping rather than succumbing, the underlying philosophy of personal adjustment training is asset-oriented. The personal adjustment trainer draws upon a variety of programs to help individuals with a disability utilize their strengths and develop values that allow them to contain the effects of disability and to open up behavioral possibilities (Wright, 1975). These behavioral possibilities ultimately become the coping responses that the individual needs in order to respond to disability-related "problems in living."

PERSONAL ADJUSTMENT TRAINING APPROACHES

Although there are many ways to categorize the coping abilities needed by rehabilitation clients, Trieschmann (1974) provided one helpful way for looking at both adjustment services and rehabilitation outcomes. In Chapter 3, Trieschmann's system for breaking rehabilitation outcomes into physical maintenance, living, and productivity categories was used for grouping personal adjustment training programs. In other words, the coping abilities that individuals need can be thought of in terms of physical maintenance skills, living skills, and productivity skills. Viewing skills in terms of certain outcome areas gives some indication of the different types of situational demands for which the individual with a disability may need skill training.

However, another way to look at skill training needed by disabled individuals is to look at the spectrum of services offered in rehabilitation, and isolate key points at which coping with disability-related problems could be facilitated. Rehabilitation adjustment services can begin with the medical or restoration needs experienced by clients during the hospital stay. During this time, adjustment training should help the client adjust to impending medical treatment. For example, the client must cope with such situational demands as an upcoming operation or some other form of anxiety-provoking medical treatment.

Another hospital-relevant situational demand has to do with the anticipatory socialization problem. Toward the end of their stay in the hospital, patients may become anxious about leaving the hospital and reentering the community. One study of problems that clients encounter in making the transition from the hospital to the community found that clients were anticipating difficulties in three main areas: problems with living arrangements, dependency problems, and adjustment to family (Bidwell, Berner, and Meier, 1972). Skill training programs responding to such areas as dependency and family adjustment are needed to prepare individuals to leave the hospital.

Another site at which rehabilitation offers adjustment skills is the rehabilitation facility. The rehabilitation facility provides skill training to improve client functioning in all three levels of Trieschmann's outcome model—self-care, living, and productivity skills. One model appropriate for facility programs, the "PIE" model, incorporates physical, intellectual, and emotional growth strategies (Carkhuff, 1971). The PIE model is also valuable because it provides an operational definition of adjustment training, i.e., services in the physical, intellectual, and emotional areas. Depending upon each individual client's situation, facilities could develop the physical, intellectual, and emotional training programs that individuals need to increase their abilities for self-care, independent living, or productivity.

In the physical area, one would find the many services offered through occupational therapy, physical therapy, recreational therapy, and physical fitness training. The contributions of physical therapy and occupational therapy to the self-care and independent living areas, as well as the productivity areas, are well known. A recent development in a related area—physical fitness (see Chapter 7)—can also be incorporated in facilitating rehabilitation outcomes. In a self-help format, physical fitness training programs enable clients to increase their levels of endurance, cardiovascular functioning, flexibility, and dynamic strength.

Intellectual skill training involves the technical skills described by Gordon (1971) as well as the many vocational skill areas. Intellectual skill training enables individuals to overcome educational deficits that held them back in the past.

The final aspect of the PIE model, emotional training, includes the emotional or personal growth programs delivered by many counseling staffs at rehabilitation facilities. These emotional and personal growth programs may be focused on adjustment to disability, interpersonal skills, self-awareness, or specific behavioral competencies.

Moving one step beyond simply looking at the kinds of training programs that clients need, adjustment training approaches can also include ways to encourage client participation in skill training experiences. In other words, two aspects of personal adjustment training exist; one being the training program itself, and the other, the system or the context in which that training program operates. In discussing the system or the context for training, one is actually looking at the rewards that exist for client participation in personal adjustment training.

Several studies have clearly demonstrated the ways in which operant conditioning techniques (that is, the use of positive and negative reinforcers, extinction, and punishment) facilitate participation in adjustment programs. These techniques can be used in conjunction with strategies to build skills in the physical, intellectual, and emotional areas. For example, operant conditioning techniques have been employed to increase performance in physical therapy, physical fitness training, and a variety of vocational and work adjustment areas. The operant (or reward) techniques may range from fairly simple systems of providing individual attention as a reward for certain desired behaviors to the complex token economies based on the use of reinforcement menus and tokens.

As the individual nears the end of the skill training phase in the facility or hospital, the concept of transition becomes extremely important. Because clients are already beginning to anticipate certain problems, it is possible to help them prepare for their transition in the hospital or facility setting. For example, pre-discharge programs exist that enable the client to live and work in the community by day and to return to the hospital in the evening for necessary supportive services.

Other models have been used to help clients make a satisfactory transition into their previous living situations. For example, one approach provides an environmental support figure at a paraprofessional level to help the individual ease into the new life situation and to reinforce or help the individual maintain behaviors established in the facility or hospital setting.

After certain transition needs have been met, the client should be somewhat stabilized and should require less individual attention than was necessary during either the hospital or the facility stay or the first few months of post-hospital or post-facility discharge. To help the individual maintain this stability, a number of specific long-term skill training programs or support programs are needed. In some cases, these programs have already been developed and utilized in rehabilitation. In other cases, the programs exist in related fields but have not been used in rehabilitation, and in some cases the need exists for the development of new programs altogether.

Long-term skill training programs that should be available to rehabilitation clients include learning the skills needed to improve sexual adjustment, marriage relationships, and child-rearing skills. Individuals also need long-term programs that enable them to improve vocational capacities and work adjustment. Finally, long-term programs can be helpful in instructing individuals in better ways to handle emotional and personal problems.

In looking at the continuum of rehabilitation services, it is obvious that personal adjustment training must begin at the pre-operation or pre-medical stage and extend through community placement. Throughout the continuum of rehabilitation services, adjustment training must identify the environmental demands that rehabilitation clients must meet, and must give clients the skills needed to meet these demands. The desired outcomes of adjustment services should be both the building of competence and the development of a feeling of success on the client's part. With both observable competencies and a feeling of success, the client will be moving toward a sense of personal mastery of the ramifications of disability.

THE HOSPITAL

Several studies have been conducted on personal adjustment training germane to the stress an individual encounters during the hospital stay. Three studies (Bradshaw and Straker, 1974; Gruen, 1975; Langer, Janis, and Wolfer, 1975) deal with efforts to help the client adjust to pre- and post-operative stress, to post-operative anxieties about his/her physical condition, and to the anxieties related to re-entry into his/her previous living situation.

Pre- and Post-operative Stress

Langer, Janis, and Wolfer (1975) studied two different approaches designed to help clients deal with their anxieties regarding an impending operation. Their adjustment strategies were based on the principle that even though the stress situation itself cannot be altered, the person's psychological reaction can be modified in several ways. For example, the person's perceived control over the aversive stimulus can be increased. The person can learn to provide distractors for the anxiety-arousing stimuli, or to acquire additional information about the threatening event.

Based on the stress reduction techniques of distraction or new information, two approaches for handling pre- and post-operative stress were examined. The first strategy was labeled a "cognitive coping device" strategy. Clients were taught to recognize the way in which attention to certain stressful cognitions increased experiential threat. Hence, clients needed to distract themselves from these anxiety-provoking thoughts and to attend selectively to something else. In the coping device procedure, clients were taught to "direct attention to the more favorable aspects of the present situation whenever they anticipated or expected discomfort" (Langer, Janis, and Wolfer, 1975, p. 156). The authors believed that the coping strategy provided an active means whereby clients could exercise some control over stress.

The other approach to handling pre- and post-operative stress was labeled the "preparatory information approach," which called for informing clients about the upcoming surgical procedure. Termed "emotional inoculation," the basic elements of the strategy included preparatory information coupled with reassurance. The authors recognized the double-edged nature of preparatory information, in that at some point the information could actually increase patient anxiety and impair the individual's coping abilities. On the other hand, a moderate level of fear would facilitate the "work of worrying," which would involve the individual in anticipatory coping, i.e., in planning what he or she would do to adjust to the situation.

After comparing the two strategies separately and together with a control condition, the authors found that the cognitive coping device lowered pre- and post-operative stress. Compared with clients in all of the other conditions, the patients in the coping device condition were rated by nurses as displaying lower anxiety and were found to have requested fewer pain relievers. As expected, the preparatory information approach seemed to cause selective attention to the surgery, and rather than calming fears, it actually raised anxieties.

The authors recommended that the coping device training be incorporated in the nurses' intake interview in order to give patients a sense of control over their own psychological reactions. Because there were several variables involved in the coping device strategy, further research was deemed necessary in order to determine what was effective about the coping strategy—the distractor, the perception of control, or both.

Recovery

Gruen (1975) examined the effects of psychotherapy on patients recovering from myocardial infarction. The basic hypothesis for the study was that psychological treatment would alter the psychological problems that the patient experienced, thereby relieving stress on a physiological level. Almost immediately upon admission to the intensive care unit, patients were seen by a counselor, whose basic approach emphasized exploration, feedback, and positive reinforcement.

Gruen (1975) broke down the counseling strategy used in working with cardiac patients into ten components: 1) the development of genuine interest in the patient, 2) reassurance to the patient that negative reactions of fear, anxiety, or depression were normal for a person in his or her situation, 3) early search for and discovery of coping mechanisms, 4) reflection of feelings and tentative conclusions emerging in psychotherapy, 5) reflection to the patient of strange or unacceptable reactions, 6) monitoring of the patient's ability to assimilate information and provision of feedback at an appropriate level, 7) encouragement of a patient's desires to get medical information from the proper sources, 8) reassurance of the therapist's faith in the patient's ability to cope, 9) encouragement of conflict resolution, and 10) constant reinforcement of coping strategies.

After comparison between a treated and a nontreated group, Gruen (1975) found that the counseling approach yielded several positive benefits; for example, the experimental group reported a shorter length of stay in the hospital and had lower incidence of congestive heart failure. Supporting the curvilinear interpretation of the effects of anxiety, a narrower (hence, more appropriate) range of anxiety was found in the experimental clients. Those clients receiving counseling were also rated as having a more surgent and vigorous mood and showed more improvement at follow-up.

Based on clinical observations, the author also noted that the counseling process developed in the Type A personality, i.e., hard-driving coronary type, a sense of perspective about past and future life. The counseling procedure also began a thought rehearsal about what the individual would do to cope with life stresses in the future. The counseling intervention also seemed to break up some of the aspects of secondary gain that were developing. In conclusion, Gruen (1975) stressed that the approach he used was appropriate for many other medical conditions.

Reentry

Bradshaw and Straker (1974) discussed an ongoing program in a Veteran's Administration (VA) hospital called the "intermediate rehabilitation unit" (IRU). The purpose of the IRU was to help patients who had improved but were not yet ready for release to prepare for the demands of independent living. The IRU focused on helping clients overcome dependency needs by gradually adapting to a more independent status in the community.

The IRU program was staffed by several social workers, nursing assistants, a secretary, and a psychiatric consultant. During their stay at the IRU, patients worked part- or full-time in the community and were encouraged to take weekend passes, join community groups, and participate in activities outside the hospital setting. Coupled with the emphasis on independent living, the IRU unit provided intensive vocational rehabilitation services in vocational training and socialization skills. The patients also learned social skills through group work at the IRU and through situations encountered in the community. Patients were discharged from the IRU only when they had met certain goals related to "self-control," "coping with independence," "accepting responsibility for self-medication," "finding and holding a job," and resolving family conflicts well enough to return home (Bradshaw and Straker, 1974, p. 165).

Of the 146 patients who were enrolled in the IRU program

(average stay—67 days), 57 did not reach all of their goals (average stay—50 days). Clients diagnosed as depressed had the most positive outcomes in terms of reaching program goals (70% successful), followed by those diagnosed as neurotic (60% successful). Goal attainment was lowest for the chronic alcoholics, with approximately one out of three (35%) reaching their goal in the program.

The authors commented on several problems that slowed client movement out of the IRU and into an independent living status. For example, many clients had multiple medical disabilities that required frequent visits back to the hospital. Also, several clients had to deal with the counter-incentive of significant VA financial benefits as long as they stayed in the VA hospital. In addition, a large percentage of the patients were not married and had no real ties to the community.

In summary, the pre/post-operative recovery and reentry programs stand as excellent examples of the way in which personal adjustment training can be incorporated into the hospital setting. These programs illustrate the feasibility of helping clients deal with the anxieties related to medical treatments like surgery, with the anxieties regarding the medical condition resulting from their sickness or disability, and with the anxieties related to returning to the community. However, the services could be more continuous if they were taken beyond the hospital walls, as in the programs to facilitate transition that are discussed later in this chapter. Before examining transition-related programs, it is necessary to look at another pre-transition setting for the delivery of personal adjustment services, the rehabilitation facility.

THE REHABILITATION FACILITY

Comprehensive facility programs to help individuals cope with the effect of disability can be described in terms of the physical, intellectual, and emotional (PIE) approach mentioned earlier in this chapter. The objectives of the PIE model are to enable clients to develop skills in key interrelated areas of daily living. The assumption is that the gains in one area will carry over to gains in the other two areas. As mentioned, the PIE model can be used to describe most facility personal adjustment training programs.

The PIE Program

A study by Roessler, Bolton, Means, and Milligan (1975) discussed the research results of a PIE training program in a comprehensive rehabilitation facility. The training program was an adjunct to the regular ongoing services provided by the Hot Springs Rehabilitation Center (Hot Springs, Arkansas). Based on an experimental/control group design, the study examined the effects of the training on indicators in the physical, intellectual, and emotional areas.

Components of the PIE program included physical fitness training, goal setting training, and interpersonal skills training. The systematic physical fitness training program focused on building up an individual's strength, endurance, and flexibility. Using a didactic approach, clients were also taught systematic goal-setting skills to apply to goals they had chosen. The interpersonal skills program helped clients improve their communication skills in terms of both discriminating and communicating at higher levels of empathy, respect, genuineness, and concreteness.

Results of the study, which are outlined in Chapter 7, showed that the training was related to definite gains in physical fitness, interpersonal skills, and goal setting. Because there was little reason to expect change on those variables unless the client had undergone systematic training, there were no control group comparisons provided for the fitness, interpersonal skills, and goal-setting measures. However, when comparing the experimental with the control group on other variables in the self-evaluation domain, there was some indication of gain for the experimental group. For example, experimental males, when compared to control males, gained significantly more in internal control. Females in the PIE program tended to improve on behavior ratings more than females in the control group.

The PIE study represents a good example of a comprehensive and systematic approach to personal adjustment training that helps clients overcome many of the skill deficits that they bring to the rehabilitation center. Of course, additional evaluation is needed to replicate the results of the initial PIE study and to determine what the effects might be of more intensive training.

Other Comprehensive Approaches

Other comprehensive approaches to personal adjustment training have been reported. For example, Gavales (1966) looked at the effects of coupling vocational training with intensive individual counseling. The basic model that he used was consistent with many facility programs that unite personal adjustment training with vocational rehabilitation.

Provided in one or more sessions per month, counseling for clients was aimed at developing employability. The counselor stressed traits related to successful employment, such as personal adjustment, reliability, dependability, honesty, loyalty, acceptance of authority, punctuality, and attentiveness.

Although there were several problems in the research methodology of the study, the treatment effect did show positive gains for the counseled group. Unfortunately, the study was replete with methodological problems such as lack of a control group, unreliability of instruments, and confusion as to which variable might be causing treatment effects, e.g., vocational training, counseling, or financial assistance while in training.

Zisfein and Rosen (1973, 1974) reported on the development of a comprehensive approach to skill training with the mentally retarded entitled "Personal Adjustment Training." The content of the structured curriculum of Personal Adjustment Training was derived from follow-up surveys regarding the problems that mentally retarded clients experienced in living in the community. Training emphasized provision of feedback and peer support coupled with a behavior therapy approach to teaching discrete coping behaviors. The curriculum contains five basic units: 1) self-evaluation, identity, and self-concept, 2) acquiescence-exploitation (the reduction of complaint behaviors in coercive situations), 3) assertiveness training, 4) heterosexual training, and 5) independence leadership training (learning to make decisions and solve problems) (Zisfein and Rosen, 1973, pp. 16–19).

In an evaluation of Personal Adjustment Training, Zisfein and Rosen (1974) found some change in behavioral measures of the skills being taught. Although they found no changes in self-evaluation, they did note that there were problems with the appropriateness of their instruments. Group leaders saw training as beneficial for clients and noted many individual gains that occurred as a function of Personal Adjustment Training.

Aspects of the PIE Model

Several studies have been completed on aspects of the PIE model. For example, Bolton and Milligan (1976) and Collingwood (1972a) reported research results of a systematic physical fitness training program with clients at the Hot Springs Rehabilitation Center. Both studies noted significant gains in physical functioning, and in one case (Collingwood, 1972a), the gains in physical functioning actually carried over into improvement in the self-evaluation of the clients. A more detailed presentation of physical fitness training is presented in Chapter 7.

Another approach to personal adjustment training emphasizing an aspect of the PIE model is represented in the Personal Achievement Skills program, which stresses both communication skills and goal setting skills. Used in a variety of settings (Roessler, Cook, and Lillard, 1977; Roessler, Milligan, and Ohlson, 1976), the Personal Achievement Skills program represents a structured group counseling approach that incorporates systematic skill training with the positive benefits of group cohesion. The Personal Achievement Skills program is discussed in more detail in Chapter 6, which describes the training and provides an overview of related research.

SUPPORT SYSTEMS FOR PERSONAL ADJUSTMENT TRAINING

Operant Conditioning

Several studies (Goodkin, 1966; Trombly, 1966; Trotter and Inman, 1968) have focused on ways to increase physical, intellectual, and emotional gains. In particular, these studies looked at the use of operant conditioning techniques to increase the incidence of desired behavior in physical, intellectual, and emotional areas. The basic learning principles employed were reinforcement, extinction, discrimination, generalization, and counter-conditioning (Trotter and Inman, 1968).

Goodkin (1966) listed three steps for using operant conditioning techniques:

1. Observe and quantify the client's mode of responding to the task in question
2. Specifically define a response class of behaviors to be accelerated and a class of behaviors to be decelerated
3. Find available reinforcers and punishers capable of altering these behaviors (p. 172).

Trotter and Inman (1968) and Trombly (1966) discussed the use of these techniques for increasing client participation in physical therapy. For example, selective reinforcement and feedback techniques were effective in increasing upper torso strength of paraplegic clients (Trotter and Inman, 1968) and in improving their use of assistive devices such as hand splints (Trombly, 1966).

Trotter and Inman (1968) also noted how important it is to relate the behavioral gains made in physical therapy to other important rehabilitation goals. Hence, the key feature of these studies included reinforcement, extinction, and feedback, along with relating behavioral gains to rehabilitation goals important to the individual.

Goodkin (1966) reported some interesting case studies in the use of operant conditioning. He discussed the case of a woman with paralysis of the right extremities who decided to learn to use the key punch with her nondominant hand. Because her initial progress on the key punch machine was extremely slow, an operant conditioning procedure was instituted.

Consistent with the three behavior principles previously mentioned, Goodkin's (1966) first step was to assess the woman's base rate of performance on the key punch machine for two days. Next, a training procedure was begun that included telling the client that she was doing well and giving her constant feedback regarding the number of seconds required to complete a card. When she performed the task faster, she was told the number of seconds cut off of her previous best time. If she performed the task slower, she was simply told to go on to the next card. Remarkable gains were charted in her key punching speed.

Similar procedures were also used to encourage an older female client to propel her wheelchair. Again, with the selective use of positive attention and feedback, client use of the wheelchair was increased considerably. In commenting on the case, Goodkin (1966) noted that operant conditioning techniques are particularly appropriate for increasing the speed of responding, decreasing the frequency of undesirable responses, and increasing the frequency of desirable responses.

In working with skill training and personal adjustment models, it is clear how the operant conditioning techniques can provide a supportive subsystem. They can actually be used to increase the incidence of desirable behaviors and decrease the incidence of undesirable behaviors. Coupling that external reinforcement with the client's own self-mediated reinforcement provides a valuable motivational force in adjustment training.

However, there are other aspects to developing a supportive system for personal adjustment training that are not at the individual client behavior level, but rather at the organizational level. Organizational aspects can have a significant effect on personal adjustment training outcomes.

Organizational Support

Several suggestions for improving the delivery of personal adjustment services emerged from a study involving the spinal cord injured at a comprehensive rehabilitation facility (Roessler, Milligan, and Ohlson, 1976). During the course of the study, attendance problems on the part of the clients were noted again and again. Reasons for missing personal adjustment training sessions included medical problems and equipment problems (see Chapter 4).

One way to overcome problems related to poor attendance would be to screen clients to be sure they are medically stable before involving them in personal adjustment programs. However, attendance in the program was also dependent upon staff commitment to the personal adjustment training program, family problems, and the release of the student when he or she had completed other programs at the center, such as vocational training and physical or occupational therapy. In other words, clients were sent home after they had completed the vocational or physical aspects of their program, regardless of where they were in their personal adjustment program. Hence, there must be a total facility commitment to the adjustment program if clients are to learn the skills they will need to make a successful transition into independent living.

TRANSITION

The first phase of independent living is the transition phase. During this phase, the client is moving for the first time from an institutional setting back into the community setting. The transition is successfully completed when the client is using the skills he or she has learned in personal adjustment training programs in facilities to meet the environmental demands of his/her life situation. Although the obvious objective of the transition is the maintenance of behavior change from one setting to the other, many clients have difficulties adjusting to different reinforcement patterns outside the institution (Walker et al., 1973). Too often, the experience is a discontinuous one in terms of reinforcements and expectations, which actually leads to a decrease in desired behaviors. Hence, there is a need to develop ways in which positive behavior change can be supported through the initial transition phase.

One approach for easing the movement from facility to home draws on the services of a trained rehabilitation mental health worker (Davidoff, Lauga, and Walzer, 1969). The concept of a rehabilitation mental health worker emerged as a response to the problem of limited resources available for aftercare work. In this approach to aftercare services, Davidoff, Lauga, and Walzer (1969) carefully screened mature mothers who could perform in a paraprofessional role working with chronic mentally ill patients. These paraprofessionals were then responsible for their client's rehabilitation in four areas: 1) social contacts and personal interactions, 2) personal habits and management of problems of daily living, 3) work adjustment, and 4) living arrangements. Each of the paraprofessionals had direct access to a team of specialists for consultation.

The mental health rehabilitation paraprofessionals worked in the community to help their clients solve problems and resist returning to previously ineffective behavior patterns. For the most part, counseling was delivered on a one-to-one basis; however, some of the paraprofessionals actually led groups in the community.

Of course, the importance of maintenance of behavior change has long been recognized in rehabilitation, as evidenced in the follow-up and follow-along concepts in rehabilitation counseling. If anything, the maintenance emphasis has been enhanced in the past few years with the enactment of the Rehabilitation Act of 1973, with its sections on post-employment services. Post-employment services are to support personal adjustment and vocational gains that might be threatened by disability-related problems after placement.

Hence, transition services help clients establish and maintain patterns of behavior contributing to long-term adjustment. However, there are also long-term adjustment programs that can be used to reinforce further gains solidified during the transition phase.

LONG-TERM ADJUSTMENT PROGRAMS

Long-term approaches for maintaining personal adjustment can be developed for three crucial areas: 1) home and family, 2) job, and 3) self-maintenance (monitoring self to avoid returning to previous ineffective behavior patterns). Home and family needs include sexual counseling, interpersonal relationship skills in marriage, and parent education for child rearing. In several cases, these programs are available through a variety of community and religious organizations and agencies. However, there is a need for more specific development of these programs as a part of long-term personal adjustment training.

Long-term approaches to vocational training set in the community have also been discussed. Calling for instant placement, Newman (1970) discussed a system in which the client moves directly from preliminary counseling to a job setting. To set up such a system, a rehabilitation counselor must contract with an industry for a given number of positions. These positions are then put under the supervision of a staff of paraprofessionals who are responsible both for assisting in the vocational training and adjustment of the clients and for guaranteeing that certain production quotas will be met. In some cases, the paraprofessionals themselves may go to work in order to meet a production quota.

Working in a realistic setting, clients begin to develop a sense of self-worth, which is reinforced through the receipt of a paycheck. Furthermore, a bond develops between the counselor and the client because of the client's realization that the counselor did, in fact, deliver—he/she got the client a job. Another important aspect of this program is that the clients are now working under the supervision of people very similar to those they will meet on the job. This more realistic behavior setting allows both the paraprofessional workers and the rehabilitation counselors to look at how the client responds to a variety of job demands. Where deficiencies in work adjustment behaviors are found, the client and counselor can work to develop a program leading to more effective work behaviors.

In the personal growth area, Solomon, Berzon, and Davis (1970) developed a leaderless group counseling program using audiotapes and participant workbooks. The leaderless program was aimed at increasing participant self-awareness of: 1) feelings, 2) how feelings affect behavior, 3) how behavior affects another's feelings, 4) how another's feelings affect one's behavior, and 5) how another's behavior affects one's feelings (Solomon, Berzon, and Davis, 1970, p. 429). The leaderless program involves a series of nine two-hour sessions. The sessions include: 1) orientation, 2) paraphrasing and self-appraisal, 3) listening laboratory, 4) description of self and other individuals, 5) feeling pooling and emotion giving, 6) emotion reporting and free session, 7) secret pooling, 8) confrontation, and 9) self-appraisal and going home.

In a research study of the leaderless group program, Solomon, Berzon, and Davis (1970) found that the training was related to increased self-esteem, self-disclosure, and motivation to work. In all, the authors concluded that the "results supported the use of the program materials in self-directed groups as a means to enhance personal growth" (Solomon, Berzon, and Davis, p. 450).

Of course, many long-term adjustment programs have a considerable history, e.g., Alcoholics Anonymous. Other similar types of programs, such as Recovery Incorporated (Dean, 1971), have also appeared in the recent literature. Dean discussed the way in which the Recovery Incorporated group, a self-directed therapy group, can be used to help clients overcome the stigmatizing aspects of disability.

The benefits of long-term group counseling approaches like Recovery Incorporated can be attributed to many factors. For example, such groups provide each individual with a sense of community acceptance and group identity. As in Recovery Incorporated, these long-term group counseling approaches provide clients both with an understanding of human behavior and with additional skills for diagnosing and resolving their own problems. Clients can also maintain membership in these ongoing groups for as long as they like. The positive support and constructive feedback from others helps to maintain many of the behavioral gains that originated at the facility or transition stages.

SUMMARY

Personal adjustment training in rehabilitation can be offered in a variety of settings to help clients learn ways to respond positively to problems in living. These problems in living may fall in such areas as physical care, independent living, or productivity. The many settings for personal adjustment training include: hospital, rehabilitation facility, transition, home, and job. Studies conducted in hospital settings included: 1) helping patients deal with the anxiety regarding treatment or surgery, 2) helping clients adjust to the physical effects of illness or disability, and 3) helping clients make a positive reentry into the community after hospital treatment. The facility treatment program was discussed in terms of physical, intellectual, and emotional gains. Based on the PIE program, systematic training approaches that provide clients with the skills needed to overcome deficits in personal functioning were covered. Systems must also be developed to support the accomplishment of personal adjustment gains in hospital and facility settings. Support for personal adjustment can come through specific client-oriented techniques, such as operant conditioning, and through organizational changes that are needed, such as more careful screening for and more staff commitment to the adjustment program. To maintain adjustment skills learned at the hospital or facility level, clients require support during the transition phase. As the individual moves from an institutional to a community setting, there are a variety of ways to provide help. Needs for personal adjustment training also extend to long-term concerns regarding home, job, and self-maintenance. Although little has been done in rehabilitation in the area of family living, there are a number of programs available for parent education through voluntary and religion-oriented organizations. Finally, long-term personal adjustment training offered through leaderless groups and group programs like Alcoholics Anonymous and Recovery Incorporated provide the individual with a sense of community and group identification throughout the period of redeveloping community ties.

Chapter 6

Personal
Achievement Skills

Research and experience in personal adjustment training in rehabilitation indicate that clients are seriously deficient in both socialization and motivational skills (Bolton, 1976; Gordon, 1971; Roessler, 1972). In addition to their physical or mental disability, rehabilitation clients are handicapped further by their lack of personal adjustment and problem-solving skills in a success- and work-oriented middle class society. Therefore, such skills must be provided through personal adjustment training programs in rehabilitation facilities. Although group counseling is the mode often selected for introducing clients to new personal and social skills, rehabilitation counselors are not always well prepared for such group counseling responsibilities.

Because some counselors have limited preparation for group work with clients, systematic group training packages have been developed (Lasky, Dell Orto, and Marinelli, 1977; Means and Roessler, 1976). These packaged approaches enable leaders to follow prescribed procedures and activities to accomplish the objectives of group counseling.

The desirability of a group counseling approach is based on a number of significant factors (Roessler, Means, and Cook, 1977). For example, group work, with its ratio of several clients to one counselor, is sound from a cost-benefit point of view. Scheduling concerns regarding personal adjustment services are relieved because group work can be assigned to predetermined time blocks. In addition to these administratively oriented factors, the significance of client interaction and mutual learning in group models can not be overlooked.

This chapter describes in detail one systematic "package" approach to group counseling that has been adopted in several rehabilitation facilities, e.g., the Hot Springs Rehabilitation Center (Hot

Springs, Arkansas), Arkansas Enterprises for the Blind (Little Rock, Arkansas), and the Criss Cole Rehabilitation Center for the Blind (Austin, Texas). Evaluation data regarding the Personal Achievement Skills program (Means and Roessler, 1976; Roessler and Means, 1976a, 1976b) are discussed after the presentation of the program.

PERSONAL ACHIEVEMENT SKILLS TRAINING (PAS) PACKAGE

Personal Achievement Skills Training takes a "treatment through training" approach to social and motivational skill building. After teaching the concepts didactically, PAS moves to activities in which members practice the new skills in a group setting. Through group feedback, individuals get a better understanding of the impact of their behavior on others and, therefore, learn how to modify their behavior in order to become more effective in real life situations.

Major life skills introduced during the course of the training include:

1. Communication Skills—how to interact with people in a positive, helpful manner
2. Self-Examination Skills—how to facilitate self-understanding and promote helpful feedback from and to others
3. Value Clarification Skills—how to examine needs and desires and translate them into meaningful personal goals
4. Valuing Skills—how to identify and utilize personal value priorities in goal selection
5. Goal Definition Skills—how to define a personal goal or objective so that it is obtainable
6. Problem Exploration Skills—how to examine the factors that have interfered or are interfering with movement toward a desired goal
7. Program Development Skills—how to schedule a series of activities and steps to achieve a goal

Perhaps the most important outcome that results from Personal Achievement Skills Training is captured in the phrase "intervention in the rut." Because people tend to fall into habitual life patterns, they occasionally need to examine and discuss where they are and where they are heading. In PAS, participants compare present and future directions with what they want to achieve in their lives. Often, the comparison creates a discrepancy that can be resolved by applying PAS to achieving personal goals.

Philosophically, PAS objectives have their roots in the interpersonal skills training and psychological education models. For example, Ivey and Alschuler (1973) outlined the following objectives for psychological education:

1. To increase individual intentionality through long- and short-term life planning skills
2. To encourage the expression of individual potential and creativity through establishing a facilitative and action-oriented environment
3. To involve many, rather than a few, in constructive, group helping experiences
4. To integrate eclectic procedures (e.g., the principles of insight and action counseling) in order to achieve goal attainment
5. To simplify, and thereby demystify, helping by making it concrete and explicit, so that participants can assimilate and transfer to others what they have learned
6. To change institutional practices, making them more democratic and individualized

Accomplishment of these objectives through PAS leads to some major changes in the lives of rehabilitation clients. For example, after completing the life planning and problem-solving exercises in PAS, one group of rehabilitation clients selected the following personal goals:

1. Control my temper
2. Be less shy
3. Be able to form close relationships
4. Be able to speak without being nervous
5. Be able to trust others
6. Be less defensive
7. Be a better listener

In order to understand how clients reached these goals, some explanation of the program is needed.

PAS has two basic purposes: 1) to teach communication and goal-setting skills, and 2) to facilitate personal growth. To accomplish these purposes, specific client-training experiences are linked in a logic consistent with the basis of effective helping—facilitation of trust, self-exploration, self-understanding, and constructive action (Carkhuff, 1969). The following list is an overview of the program model in terms of the sequence in which skills are presented:

Self-Exploration

1. Building group cohesion—involves exercises to build group rapport and trust
2. Communication lessons—includes basic elements of effective interpersonal skills
3. Value clarification—focuses on value clarification exercises of Simon and Raths

Self-Understanding

4. Valuing and goal defining—presents Lasswell's eight needs system and Rucker's approach to problem solving and decision making
5. Program development—based on the self-modification principles of Watson and Tharp and the behavioral counseling principles of Krumboltz and Thoresen
6. Goal attainment scaling—introduces Kiresuk's approach to systematic goal attainment evaluation

Constructive Action

7. Monitoring—periodic monitoring of participant progress toward goal attainment
8. Goal attainment—achievement of a personal goal
9. Continued use of skills—application of Personal Achievement Skills to additional life goals

PAS is divided into two essential elements: the social phase and the motivational phase. The social phase of the program includes exercises for building group cohesion and lessons in effective communication. The motivational phase of the program focuses on goal attainment through specific exercises and activities aimed at value clarification, goal setting, and goal achievement.

Social Phase

Initially, participants complete activities that make them feel comfortable with the group and the leader. During the group cohesion exercises, participants learn how to reveal personal feelings and experiences, which they continue to practice under facilitative conditions. Facilitative conditions allow participants to reveal what they feel comfortable sharing about themselves and their goals. As trust in the group builds, participants deal with progressively more meaningful information about themselves.

The series of activities and exercises to build group cohesion includes:

1. The PAS group leader communicates unconditional caring and respect during the introduction of the program.
2. The PAS group leader creates a need for personal revelation by explaining and demonstrating how it is a necessary step in behavior change.
3. The group discusses two poems that communicate the idea that most people want to be more open but find it very difficult.
4. The leader introduces PAS ground rules: a) everyone belongs here, b) confidentiality, c) our personal goal is growth, d) our commitment to others is to be helpful, e) we are not judgmental about another person's goals or values, f) we try to be honest in terms of what we think and feel, g) decisions made by the group require everyone's participation, and h) before quitting the group, a participant must give the group 20 minutes. The leader asks if there are any ground rules the participants would like to add.
5. Participants share their values, goals, and self-perceptions through the following exercises: "Who are you?" and "How do others see me?"

As participants begin to feel open with one another and get the feel of self-exploration, the leader introduces the concept of effective communication. In the PAS program, effective communication skills are taught through several lessons based on key features of the interpersonal skills training program. Preceding the goal-setting section, the communication lessons include the following:

1. What not to do:
   hate
   advise
   change
2. What to do:
   attend
   listen
   respond
3. Effective communication:
   the caring response

Ineffective communication is illustrated in the first three lessons, focusing on hating, advising, and changing responses. The next set of lessons, through examples and role playing, helps participants identify effective communication approaches. The final lesson emphasizes avoiding the aspects of poor communication—

hating, advising, and changing—and concentrating on responding to what other people are feeling and thinking and why they are feeling and thinking that way.

Use of the communication skills and participation in cohesion exercises contributes to a facilitative group atmosphere, the foundation for meaningful exploration, understanding, and action regarding a personal goal. As group members begin to trust one another and help one another, they are increasingly able to explore their values and goals. This meaningful self-exploration increases the probability that participants will honestly assess themselves and will select goals that they need to accomplish to become more effective in their personal lives.

Motivational Phase

Motivational training builds from the foundation of interpersonal skills and group cohesion in two ways. As mentioned, the feeling of trust and rapport that builds in the group increases the possibility of meaningful self-exploration. Secondly, significant self-exploration gradually evolves into the two other phases of the PAS program model, self-understanding and constructive action, which are two key elements of the motivational or intentionality phase of Personal Achievement Skills Training.

To develop intentionality, PAS integrates the procedures of value clarification, goal defining, problem exploration skills, program development, and goal attainment scaling. In PAS, increased intentionality includes two concepts: *goal selection* and *goal achievement.*

Goal Selection   Goal selection does not mean deciding to work toward just any goal (Winter, Griffith, and Kolb, 1968). The goal must be a valued one, in the sense that it was selected from a set of meaningful personal goals. To generate a set of significant goals, participants complete a series of value clarification exercises similar to those developed by Simon, Howe, and Kirschenbaum (1972). These activities are designed to start each participant in the group thinking about such questions as:

Who are you?
What are some things you have accomplished?
What are some things you want to accomplish?
What do you need to do that you are not doing?
What are you doing that you need to improve on?

Are you using your time and energy in the way you want to use
them?

When will you start working on your goal?

Self-exploration ends when participants have clarified some
potential goals and recognized the discrepancy these goals represent,
i.e., these goals represent things participants say they *want* to do but
have not yet done. Participants share their potential goals with the
group and then begin to consider selecting one goal to focus on
during Personal Achievement Skills Training. Goal selection introduces the phase of self-understanding.

To help them select one goal to concentrate on, participants
complete several exercises. One exercise focuses on increasing an
individual's understanding of his/her own values and priorities.
Additional exercises enable the participant to contrast potential
goals with value priorities. After feedback from the group and the
leader, each participant selects a tentative goal and moves to the
next phase of self-understanding, goal sharpening.

Goal sharpening skills include thinking skills (Rucker, Arnspiger, and Brodbeck, 1969) and valued decision criteria (Raths,
Harmin, and Simon, 1966). The thinking skills aspect introduces
participants to steps in problem solving and, basically, involves
participants in exploring the history of their goals.

To proceed through the problem-solving sequence, participants
respond to the group leader, the group, and their participant workbooks in terms of the following issues:

Goal thinking:	What is my goal?
	Is it a real problem?
Trend thinking:	What conditions in the past have helped or hindered me in achieving my goal?
Condition thinking:	What conditions in the present can help or hinder me in achieving my goal?
Projective thinking:	If I let events take their natural course and do nothing special, can I still achieve my goal?
Alternative thinking:	What alternative ways exist to achieve my goal?
	(Rucker, Arnspiger, and Brodbeck, 1969).

As participants consider questions of goal, trend, condition, and
projective thinking, they gradually sharpen their own goals and are
ready to turn to the final phase of thinking skills, alternative thinking.
Alternative thinking raises two issues for participants, alternative
development and choice making.

PAS stresses the importance of freedom and imagination in alternative development. In generating alternative solutions, participants should allow themselves to consider solutions that range from the impossible to the possible. They can select from among these later; for now, it is important that they not arbitrarily limit their alternatives. For example, some people are more concerned about what others think than about their own feelings and needs. Emphasis in the PAS group is on helping each other create and explore a wide range of alternatives.

Because a wide range of alternatives can immobilize a person, the next phase of Personal Achievement Skills Training provides insights into a decision-making strategy based on Raths' value criteria (Raths, Harmin, and Simon, 1966). Raths' system stresses that a person has arrived at a valued decision if he or she can respond positively to each of the following questions:

Choosing:	Did you choose freely?
	Did you choose from alternatives?
	Did you examine the consequences of each alternative?
Prizing:	Are you proud of your choice?
	Would you recommend it for others?
Acting:	Are you acting repeatedly in some pattern?

If participants can respond affirmatively to the Choosing and Prizing questions from Raths' scheme, they are ready to consider the Acting question, "Are you acting on it repeatedly in some pattern?"

Before considering the acting question, it is important to have participants make a public commitment to their goal and to their valued alternative for reaching that goal (Winter, Griffith, and Kolb, 1968). This public commitment is followed by emphasis on behavioral specifications of the goal, a procedure that involves clients in specifying problem behaviors—behaviors they want to decrease—and resolution behaviors—behaviors they want to increase. The process for identifying problem and resolution behaviors is called "behavior analysis," and occurs as a group exercise after clients have participated in the extensive self-exploration and self-understanding exercises that have resulted in identification of a goal they want to accomplish.

The basis for the exercise is the completion of a behavior analysis sheet, which begins by involving each participant in examining reasons for personal dissatisfaction. The incomplete sentence, "I am dissatisfied because I am ____," is given, and usually some kind of trait label is used to complete it. For example, one PAS client described herself as "too impatient."

The next step of behavior analysis involves identifying cues or situational factors eliciting the trait label. In the case of the "impatient" client, the situation eliciting dissatisfaction was one in which she was interrupted while doing something she wanted to complete.

Next, the individual specifies the behaviors associated with the stimulus situation. For example, when interrupted, the "impatient" client first behaved internally in ways not matched by her overt behavior. She gave no indication of her inner thoughts and feelings of irritation in her overt smiling and attending behavior, which served to encourage the interruption. If other people had extra-sensory perception, they might have heard the client say to herself, "You dummy, can't you see I have to work?"

Because behavior analysis focuses on a chain of events, the next step deals with how the other person reacts or responds to the client's behavior. In the case of the interrupted client, the other person, having only her overt behaviors to respond to, continues to interrupt, causing an increase in the internal irritation experienced by the client.

The next link in the chain is to examine how the client reacts to the other person's actions. Our client wrote that she began to act in ways that she hoped would convey the message, "I can't stop now." She would avoid eye contact, return to her studies or work, make cutting remarks, and in other ways actively ignore the other person.

Her attempts to terminate the interruption were often ineffective and misinterpreted, and led her to feel more unhappy and depressed—a feeling that resulted in her labeling herself as "inconsiderate and impatient." The behavioral analysis clearly illustrated the vicious cycle the client faced. The way to break the cycle involved examining what she would have to do to be satisfied. Again, the analysis began with a trait label. For our example client, the satisfaction label was one of "being patient or considerate."

Because the client could not infallibly exercise stimulus control (that is, remove interrupting situations from her life) the problem situation remained the same—being interrupted while working. However, she was now planning to respond to the interrupting situation with new behaviors. As Mischel (1973) pointed out, these self-regulatory systems and plans are important aspects of "person" variables that can influence behavior.

The client now began to plan how she would like to act when interrupted. She identified the following steps:

1. Stop and analyze the situation—a good step for delaying impulsive behavior according to Skinner (1953).
2. Decide whether or not the interruption is important enough for me to stop my work; if so, stop and attend fully to the person.
3. If not, say "I really need to finish this work. I promised myself I would work two hours on it. Could we get together later?"

She felt that the other person would accept her wishes. Of course, she also planned to follow-up on any commitments made.

The key feature of behavior analysis is that it involves individuals in analyzing a problem situation, and, with the help of others, planning new responses to that situation. Having been helped to be operationally specific, clients move from the abstract level of trait attribution to answering questions such as why, when, what, and how. For example:

1. Why are you dissatisfied?
2. When are you dissatisfied?
3. What do you do?
4. How does the other person react?
5. How do you feel?
6. What can you do to feel satisfied?

Following the leads provided by behavior analysis, clients develop plans that help them to see themselves as more effective, however that may be defined, which gives rise to good feelings about how they are now handling problem situations.

Goal Achievement   After behavior analysis, Personal Achievement Skills Training moves to other self-understanding techniques to increase individual self-control, e.g., program development (Houts and Scott, 1972) and goal attainment scaling (Kiresuk, Salasin, and Garwick, 1972). Program development is based on specific answers to the following questions:

1. Is your goal meaningful, manageable, and measurable?
2. What steps must you take to reach your goal?
3. What specific behaviors or actions are involved in each step?
4. Have you selected dates when you expect to complete each step?
5. What results do you expect from each step?
6. What are the actual results of each step? (Houts and Scott, 1972).

After discussing these questions in the group, participants begin to develop programs for achieving their goals. With the help of the leader, the group, and other resources, participants complete a program development form by specifying steps, deadlines, and anticipated results for their program. Participants work on the program development form until they, the group, and the leader feel that the program is a sound one.

The last phase of self-understanding introduces participants to goal attainment scaling (Kiresuk, Salasin, and Garwick, 1972), a procedure for evaluating the effectiveness of goal-directed behavior. Goal attainment scaling involves participants in specifying outcome levels for their goals, ranging in degree of success and failure from the best possible outcome to the worst possible outcome.

The goal attainment scaling exercise helps participants clarify their goals. Also, participants can talk about their feelings regarding each outcome of the goal attainment scale, e.g.:

Do participants really want to reach their expected attainment level?
Are participants afraid of failing, of reaching their worst possible outcome?
Would participants be willing to try for more than their expected outcome?

Goal attainment scaling also stresses the importance of the program: "Follow it, and you are likely to reach your expected goal level; deviate from it, and you are likely to reach a less-than-expected goal level." Finally, and most importantly for the next phase, constructive action, goal attainment scaling provides a way to evaluate goal attainment efforts.

As they follow their program development form during the constructive action phase of the program, participants and the leader need to know how goal attainment is proceeding, and, indeed, when it has occurred. In other words, have participants reached their expected outcome, best possible outcome, or worst possible outcome? Questions relevant to following one's program and evaluating goal attainment are central to the constructive action phase of the PAS program.

The final phase of Personal Achievement Skills Training is constructive action—acting repeatedly on one's goal. As stressed in the interpersonal skills model, appropriate action can come only when a person has explored and understood his/her problem. In PAS, participants can act on their goals only after exploration and understanding of what they want to do.

With their program development form and their goal attainment scale, participants are ready to act, to pursue their goals step-by-step for four to six weeks. During the action phase, follow-up sessions are held to discuss each participant's progress toward his or her goal. A special worksheet helps participants and the leader focus on goal attainment efforts and goal attainment status. These worksheets also serve as a basis for group discussion of participant goal attainment efforts.

For example, the Goal Attainment Worksheets include the following exercises and questions:

1.   Describe your present progress toward your goal.
2.   Rate your progress toward goal attainment (where are you now—moving toward best possible, expected, worst possible).
3.   How do you feel about your progress toward your goal?
4.   What have you learned about your goal attainment program?
5.   What do you wonder about in terms of your goal, your program, yourself, etc.?

In one sense, Personal Achievement Skills Training never comes to an end; participants should continue to use the social and motivational skills throughout their lives. In terms of the original program intent, the actual group experience should end after several weeks in the constructive action phase. The final meeting of the group focuses on each participant's progress toward his or her goal. Those who have reached their goals can serve as models for those who need to continue with their program development forms.

It is also important that the group leader be available to those who want to continue with their goal programs. In addition, the group should plan to meet again in about six to eight weeks for a final review of participant progress toward goal attainment.

Use of PAS Package

Overall, PAS spans activities ranging from problem identification to reinforcement of behavior change. Accomplishing PAS objectives requires that the program be conducted by a trained leader in a comfortable, private setting appropriate for small groups. Although scheduling of PAS groups can vary, it is suggested that sessions run from 90 to 120 minutes and be held two to three times a week. Experience indicates that the training phase requires about 40 hours. After the training period, the group should meet periodically to discuss progress and problems related to self-directed achievement. These weekly meetings provide an opportunity to monitor individual goal progress.

To facilitate use of PAS, a self-instructional, packaged approach has been followed. Materials for the program include a Leader's Manual, a Participant's Workbook, supplementary program materials, and group instructional tapes, all of which are available from the Arkansas Rehabilitation Research and Training Center.

To gain first-hand experience with PAS, prospective group leaders can participate in the Arkansas Rehabilitation Research and Training Center's workshop. After completing the workshop, they should study the Leader's Manual thoroughly and review the sequence of exercises in the Participant's Workbook. Due to the systematic, skill-based approach to PAS, leaders need only a relatively brief introduction to the program before beginning to conduct the program in their own agencies and facilities.

One-to-one applications of the techniques in Personal Achievement Skills Training are discussed in Chapter 8. The PAS program has resulted from a series of pilot studies and evaluation studies that are discussed in the following section.

Research Review

Personal Achievement Skills Training has a long developmental history. The earliest efforts (1973–1974), conducted at the University of Arkansas and the Hot Springs Rehabilitation Center, concentrated on developing a logical sequence of training activities that participants enjoyed. The next step involved introducing the program to rehabilitation personnel involved in personal adjustment training (February 1974). As a result of this training program, Personal Achievement Skills Training was implemented at the Criss Cole Rehabilitation Center for the Blind (Austin, Texas), where the positive reception from clients stimulated the later modification of PAS for the visually handicapped. Additional PAS research was conducted with rehabilitation counselors, high school students, and work adjustment clients.

Rehabilitation counselors who were members of the Arkansas Chapter of the National Rehabilitation Counselors Association participated in a PAS leader training session (June 1974). Evaluating the program favorably, participants commented that the program helped them both personally and professionally. They felt that rehabilitation clients would profit from involvement in Personal Achievement Skills Training (Roessler and Green, 1974).

Other analyses of the evaluation data indicated that each group leader was rated positively for his or her skill in leading PAS groups. However, there was some indication that leaders with more experience with the program were more effective trainers than those with less experience.

Another research activity (Roessler and DeWeese, 1975) with PAS involved high school students in completing the program as a credited course sponsored by the high school guidance department. Led by a high school teacher with experience in Personal Achievement Skills Training, the program was part of the regular curriculum offering of the high school. Students attended for one hour a day, five days a week, for an entire school semester.

At the end of the course, most students (91%) either achieved their goal (41%) or made noticeable progress toward it (50%). Teacher and aide observations, coupled with written comments from student's evaluations, underscored observations from other programs to the effect that Personal Achievement Skills Training contributes to personal growth by providing participants:

1. A better understanding of their personal responsibility for their own behavior
2. A recognition that behavior is a manifestation of personal values
3. An awareness of the multiple decisions an individual makes and the ramifications of those decisions
4. Some insight into the need for a reality base—strengths, limitations, risks, opportunities, etc.—in personal decision making
5. An appreciation of the role personal commitment plays in goal attainment

Although possibly a function of regression to the mean, self-esteem tended to increase for PAS participants.

The most extensive study of Personal Achievement Skills Training in an applied setting was in the work adjustment program at the Hot Springs Rehabilitation Center (Roessler, Cook, and Lillard, 1976, 1977). The subjects for the study were young and of average intelligence, and had been referred to work adjustment because, for the most part, they were experiencing problems in their Center training programs.

The following general statements can be made about the effectiveness of PAS as demonstrated in the work adjustment program at the Center:

1. More PAS participants than control subjects reported improve-

ment in life perspective, as measured by Cantril's Self-Anchoring Striving Scale (1965).

2. PAS participants reported significantly greater gain 'pre' to 'post' on vocational maturity, vocational functioning, and interpersonal maturity, as measured by self-report responses to the Facility Outcome Measure developed by the Program Planning and Evaluation section of Arkansas Rehabilitation Services.

3. Self-reported evidence of goal attainment occurred predominately for the PAS group.

4. Data suggested that the PAS group developed a more realistic perception of the benefits of work.

5. The PAS program was rated as useful, stimulating, and well-organized by program participants.

6. No differences were found between PAS participants and control subjects on counselor and leader ratings of current adjustment or improvement in adjustment.

Over all, clients' self-report data strongly support the use of PAS in work adjustment settings. However, the results also suggest that more attention to maintaining goal-oriented behaviors across settings in the Center is needed. With the success in the work adjustment setting, it became even more apparent that the PAS approach had potential for other rehabilitation settings.

PAS FOR THE VISUALLY HANDICAPPED

Based on the early success experiences at the Criss Cole Rehabilitation Center for the Blind, and the positive findings from several research studies, a research proposal was drafted calling for the development of a special Personal Achievement Skills Training program for the visually handicapped. Drawing on the resources of the Criss Cole Rehabilitation Center for the Blind and Arkansas Enterprises for the Blind (Little Rock, Arkansas), several pilot studies were conducted to prepare PAS materials for use with the visually handicapped. These efforts resulted in the addition of another Leader's Manual to the PAS program, *Personal Achievement Skills for The Visually Handicapped* (Roessler and Means, 1977).

With the help of counselors at the two rehabilitation centers, Personal Achievement Skills Training was modified to accomplish the objectives of the original PAS program through verbal, braille, and motor modes of presentation. No visual ability is required for clients to complete the special PAS program for the visually handicapped.

One example of the modification needed to adapt PAS for individuals with visual handicaps is found in one of the early value clarification activities, the Lifeline (Simon, Howe, and Kirschenbaum 1972). Originally, the exercise calls for an individual to mark birth date at one end of a line, expected year of one's death at the other end, and where one is right now between the two. The exercise documents visually the amount of time the individual has to attain life goals.

Because the visual approach was obviously inappropriate, the Lifeline exercise had to be changed so that it led to the same insights but without any visual inputs. A coat hanger wire and macrame beads were used to represent the Lifeline and number of years lived and to live. With each bead representing five years, the participant moves those beads needed to represent current age to the left end of the wire. Then, after sliding the remaining beads to the right end of the wire, the person returns to the middle of the wire only those beads needed to represent how many more years he or she expects to live. By spanning these beads between thumb and forefinger, the individual has an immediate awareness of the amount of time remaining to accomplish significant life goals.

Research Review

Following completion of the Leader's Manual, research regarding the impact of PAS was conducted at Arkansas Enterprises for the Blind (Roessler, 1978). The study involved 34 clients enrolled in a personal adjustment program. Of those students qualifying for the research (IQ 70 or above, braille skills, and projected 12 week enrollment in the adjustment program), 16 were in the experimental group and 18 in the control group. Subjects involved in the study could be described in the following way: male (56%), young (average age of 29), single (56%), and white (82%), with 12 years of education. Because clients were randomly assigned, no differences were found between experimental and control groups on most demographic variables, e.g., sex, race, years of education, and age when disabled. However, the control group was somewhat older (average age of 32) than the experimental group (average age of 26).

Promising results from the use of PAS with the visually handicapped were found. Although the control group was also involved in group counseling, the experimental PAS clients reported greater gains in self-esteem and trends toward higher self-report gains in goal attainment from pre- to posttesting. Initially reporting an internal locus of control, neither experimental nor control group changed significantly on Rotter's (1966) Scale of Beliefs. Based on Cantril's (1965) life ladder results, equivalent proportions of both groups reported more optimistic life perceptions (about 50% of each group).

Sample client goals from the PAS program at Arkansas Enterprises for the Blind included the following: to be more involved in social activities, to be more assertive, to be a more effective listener, to make more friends, and to be less competitive. One of the female participants in a PAS group developed the following goal program:

1. Week one—Go to recreation areas in the center rather than stay in my room
2. Week two—Go out with groups to movies, plays, etc., when asked
3. Week three—Initiate card games or other activities by asking others to join me
4. Week four—Go out to a social event with one person who invites me
5. Week six—Invite one person (male) to go out with me to do something I think we would both enjoy

Although the leader of the PAS group should help the student break these steps into smaller segments, the program cited represents successive approximation of a desirable goal that has anxiety-provoking aspects. In this case, the female group member gradually became comfortable both as a participant in and initiator of social activities.

PAS makes unique contributions to personal adjustment training in that it teaches specific skills of behavioral self-control and enables individuals to develop through the accomplishment of a personally meaningful goal. The way in which PAS accomplishes these objectives is operationalized in the exercises and activities presented in the *PAS Leader's Manual for the Visually Handicapped* (Roessler and Means, 1977). Having learned to use these activities, group leaders can provide clients with a beneficial and consistent personal adjustment training experience.

SUMMARY

Personal Achievement Skills Training (PAS) is a systematic personal adjustment training package that uses a group counseling format. After teaching the basic concepts didactically, PAS moves to a series of activities in which clients practice seven major life skills in a group setting: communication skills, self-examination skills, value clarification skills, valuing skills, goal definition skills, problem exploration skills, and program development skills. These life skills exemplify the two fundamental purposes of PAS: to learn communication and goal setting skills and to enhance personal growth. The developmental exercises that comprise the PAS package are presented in a sequence that begins with self-exploration and leads to self-understanding and strategies for constructive action. PAS generally requires about 40 hours for completion of the planned activities, which are presented in a Leader's Manual and a workbook for participants. The versatility of the PAS package is illustrated by its adaption for use with visually handicapped clients. A variety of research studies have provided empirical support for the effectiveness of PAS in improving the self-perceptions and life skills of rehabilitation clients.

Chapter 7

Physical Fitness Training

The arguments and evidence supporting the importance of physical fitness as an intermediate process goal in rehabilitation have been summarized by Collingwood (1972b). The fundamental premise underlying the implementation of physical fitness training in rehabilitation programs is outlined by him:

> How well an individual functions physically limits or extends his (or her) energy level, stamina and strength to function not just physically, but in all areas of life as well. The physical functioning of an individual is the base from which his (or her) life efforts extend—his (or her) source of energy and power. From this standpoint alone, increased physical fitness is not just important, but is a necessity for all life functioning (Collingwood, 1972b, p. 72).

The results of several research investigations indicate that increased physical fitness may foster enhanced self-esteem, a reduction in behavioral problems, and increased social effectiveness, as well as improved physical functioning. Collingwood (1972b) reviewed several studies and concluded that "... in terms of emotional functioning ... the process of becoming physically fit can be a key modality for affecting those psychosocial dimensions which in many cases, more so than disability, determine vocational rehabilitation success" (p. 73).

Physical fitness training in rehabilitation is an essential component of a comprehensive personal adjustment program. It can be viewed as a supplement to Personal Achievement Skills Training, or it can be used in conjunction with Carkhuff's (1971) human resource development model, which includes three major areas of emphasis: physical, intellectual, and emotional (the "PIE" model, which was outlined in Chapter 5). Physical fitness training can also be viewed within the context of therapeutic recreation. In addition to the general objectives of physical conditioning that were stated above, the following specific benefits of participation in recreational activities may result (Collingwood, n.d.):

1. Pleasurable participation
    The more a client participates in activities in which he/she undergoes gratifying experiences, the higher the level of morale and the greater the lessening of depression.
2. Enthusiasm
    The more active a client is, the more turned on and involved he/she becomes in his/her environment, experiences, and future.
3. Safe reality testing
    Recreational activities provide experiences in which a client can safely test reality and respond to success and failure experiences without serious consequences.
4. Accomplishment
    Regardless of activity participated in, a sense of accomplishment or achievement can occur from just participating. This sense of achievement can directly improve motivation.
5. Ego involvement
    By nature, recreational activities are involved activities at some level. From this, a healthy caring and concern for oneself emerges.
6. Skill acquisition
    At some level all recreational activities facilitate some type of skill learning. Self-esteem can emerge from successful learning experiences.
7. Socialization
    Interacting with others, following rules, cooperation, and accepting some level of responsibility is usually inherent in most recreational activities.
8. Self-expression
    Regardless of type of activity, recreation activities allow clients to more freely express their feelings. This allows them to know themselves better.
9. Self-concept
    On a general level, participation in recreational activities can aid clients to overcome self-consciousness, facilitate self-confidence and self-respect, provide opportunities for self-evaluation and expression, and facilitate the development of self-identification and self-discipline.

10. Constructive use of leisure time
    The learning of new recreation skills can generalize to construc-
    tive use of leisure time (a critical factor in the rehabilitation
    of alcoholics, drug abusers, and public offenders).

THE PHYSICAL FITNESS TRAINING [PF] PACKAGE

Despite the conclusions noted above, which are supported by some
research and centuries of experience (the "sound mind in a sound
body" philosophy), most rehabilitation facilities do not offer systematic physical training in conjunction with personal adjustment
training programs. One reason may be lack of facilities, but a more
probable reason is that, until recently, a systematic physical fitness
package for use with rehabilitation clients has not been available.

To remedy this deficiency in the rehabilitation service program,
the Physical Fitness Training (PF) package was developed by the
training faculty of the Arkansas Rehabilitation Research and
Training Center. The PF package was designed to accomplish
the following objectives:

1. It can be used in rehabilitation facilities without the addition
   of specially trained personnel.
2. It can be implemented without monetary investments in special
   equipment.
3. Client physical fitness levels are measurably increased.
4. Client motivation to maintain physical fitness is increased by
   providing health and fitness information and teaching principles
   for establishing personal fitness programs.

Components of the PF Package

The PF package consists of three major components, which are described as follows:

1. An instructor's manual (Milligan, 1976a) containing:
   a) Physical fitness evaluation procedures for assessing client
      fitness without elaborate equipment
   b) A progressive exercise program designed to increase client
      fitness levels in cardiovascular functioning, flexibility,
      endurance, and dynamic strength—exercise routines are
      individualized for different client fitness levels.

2. A participant's manual (Milligan, 1976b) for client use, containing:
   a) Personal health and fitness checklists
   b) Forms for charting daily performance in the PF program
   c) Guides for developing and implementing continuing individual fitness programs.
3. A series of 23 daily lectures on health and fitness topics (Milligan, 1976c) that are available on audio cassettes. The brief lectures focus on principles of rest, hygiene, diet, exercise, and guidelines for setting up individual fitness programs.

The PF package was designed to bring clients to minimal physical fitness levels in 20 to 25 one-hour classes. Each class includes a brief lecture on a selected topic in health and fitness, followed by a 50-minute exercise period. The exercises, which stress the development of flexibility, dynamic strength, and cardiovascular endurance, are organized in a warm-up, hard work, and taper-off format. The program is best suited for clients with minor or no mobility restrictions, i.e., it was not designed for use with lower-limb amputees, spinal cord injured clients, etc. However, the PF package is being modified for use with spinal cord injured clients; a Fitness for Paraplegics package is being developed (Milligan and Roessler, 1977). Finally, the PF package can be used effectively with both female and male clients.

Fitness Measures and Exercises

The first day of the PF program is devoted to a fitness evaluation. The purpose of the initial evaluation is to provide the instructor and each of the participants with individual benchmarks so that progress can be assessed and the exercise program can be adjusted to each client's level of fitness. On the final day, the fitness evaluation may be repeated and individual progress charted on a Personal Fitness Profile in the participant's manual.

The fitness measures are briefly described as follows:

1. Body weight
2. Cardiovascular functioning
   The step test (Waxman, 1960) requires subjects to step up and down on a bench, 12 steps for 1 minute, with pulse rate taken for 2 minutes afterwards.
3. Flexibility
   The extent to which clients can complete a toe touch exercise (Friermood, 1963) provides a measure of flexibility.

4. Endurance
   The amount of time a client requires to complete a 600-yard run constitutes the endurance measure (AAHPER, 1965).
5. Dynamic strength
   Relative level of dynamic strength is assessed by the number of sit-ups a client can complete in 2 minutes (AAHPER, 1965).

Each of the 22 classes after the fitness evaluation includes a systematic, progressive series of exercises. While the exercises are tailored to each client's needs and limitations, the basic format is the same. The typical workout consists of the following exercises:

1. Warm-up
   fast walking and jogging, arm swings (10 minutes)
2. Flexibility conditioning
   toe touch, knee pull, leg swings, cross-legged sit, sit/stretch, chest pull (5 minutes)
3. Endurance
   walk, jog, run (10 minutes)
4. Dynamic strength conditioning
   sit-ups, push-ups, toe raises, reverse sit-ups, knee bends, chair dips, pull-ups (10 minutes)
5. Endurance
   fast walking, jogging, running (10 minutes)
6. Taper-off
   slow walking, arm swings (5 minutes)

The Lecture Series

A major shortcoming of many physical training programs is the absence of a plan for ensuring continuation after the formal program terminates. The inclusion of the "cognitive" component—the 23 mini-lectures—should help the client to realize that fitness is a never-ending process that can only be maintained with a life-long exercise regime. Also, many rehabilitation clients are deficient in their knowledge of basic principles of health and personal hygiene; thus, the lectures provide information that is essential to a comprehensive personal adjustment curriculum.

The remainder of this section contains an outline of all 23 lectures in the series and the verbatim typescripts of two lectures that were selected to illustrate the content and level of presentation of the series.

Outline of Lectures

Day 1: Orientation
  1. Welcome to fitness class
  2. Purpose of fitness class
     a) Meaning of good physical health
     b) Benefits
  3. Description of class routine
  4. Explanation of the fitness test
     a) Cardiovascular fitness
     b) Flexibility
     c) Endurance
     d) Dynamic strength
  5. Assignments for next day

Day 2: Questionnaire and Familiarization with Exercises
  1. Review of previous day's assignments
  2. Rest and relaxation questionnaire
  3. Hygiene questionnaire
  4. Grooming
     a) Bathing
     b) Care of teeth
     c) Care of nails

Day 3: Relaxation Exercises
  1. Explanation of terms—rest, hygiene, diet, exercise
  2. Rest
     a) Importance of sleep
     b) Guidelines for ensuring adequate sleep
     c) Combating insomnia
  3. Next day's assignments

Day 4: High, Middle, Low Gear Groups
  1. Explanation of grouping according to fitness levels
  2. Class exercise routine
     a) 10 minutes, warm-up
     b) 5 minutes, flexibility conditioning
     c) 10 minutes, endurance
     d) 10 minutes, dynamic strength conditioning
     e) 10 minutes, endurance
     f) 5 minutes, taper-off

Day 5: Fitness Areas
  1. Listing of fitness areas to be focused on
     a) Cardiovascular functioning
     b) Circulatory functioning

    c)   Flexibility

    d)   Dynamic strength

2. Differentiate from athletics

    a)   Description of athletic fitness

    b)   Description of conditioning for health

Day 6: Cardiovascular System

1. Listing of body systems

    a)   Cardiovascular

    b)   Respiratory

    c)   Digestive

2. Description of cardiovascular system

    a)   What is included (heart, veins, arteries, capillaries)

    b)   How the system works

3. Indicators of cardiovascular efficiency

4. Importance of cardiovascular efficiency—cholesterol effect on system efficiency

Day 7: Cardiovascular Functioning

1. Heart disease—causes

    a)   Heredity

    b)   Sedentary living

    c)   Obesity

    d)   Smoking

    e)   Lack of exercise

    f)   Age

2. Importance of exercise

    a)   Reduce high blood pressure

    b)   Reduce cholesterol

3. How to exercise to improve cardiovascular efficiency

    a)   Running as the key

    b)   Progressing gradually

Day 8: Respiratory System

1. Function of the respiratory system

2. Diseases that affect the respiratory system

3. Smoking's effect on the respiratory system

4. Tips for quitting or cutting down on smoking

5. What exercise does for the respiratory system

    a)   Oxygen exchange

    b)   Aerobic exercise

Day 9: Skeletal system

1. Definition of skeletal system

    a)   Components

    b)   Function of components
  2. Measuring flexibility of skeletal system
    a)   Extent
    b)   Dynamics
  3. Exercises to increase flexibility

Day 10: Posture and Body Mechanics
  1. Importance of good posture
  2. Causes of poor posture
    a)   Skeletal misalignment
    b)   Poor muscle tone
    c)   Muscle imbalance
  3. Effects of exercise on posture

Day 11: Posture
  1. Description of good standing posture
  2. Description of good sitting posture
  3. Pushing, pulling, picking up heavy objects
  4. Carrying heavy objects

Day 12: Muscular System
  1. Voluntary muscles
    a)   Function
    b)   How they work
  2. Exercises for the muscular system
    a)   Isometric
    b)   Isotonic

Day 13: Hygiene
  1. Definition of hygiene
    a)   Personal maintenance
    b)   Guardian maintenance
  2. Areas for special attention and suggested actions:
    a)   Teeth
    b)   Hands
    c)   Total body
    d)   Hair
    e)   Feet
    f)   Underarms
    g)   Clothing

Day 14: Nutrition
  1. Good food as a source of energy
  2. Basic nutrients
    a)   Carbohydrates
    b)   Fats
    c)   Protein

     d)   Vitamins
     e)   Minerals

Day 15:   Diet
  1. Four major food groups
     a)   Milk group
     b)   Meat group
     c)   Fruit and vegetable group
     d)   Bread and cereal group
  2. Empty foods
  3. Foods that hinder fitness
     a)   Stimulants
     b)   Alcohol
     c)   Substituting empty foods for nutritious foods

Day 16:   Weight Control
  1. Causes of obesity
     a)   Eating habits
     b)   Exercise habits
     c)   Calories
  2. Fad diets
     a)   Diet pills
     b)   Low carbohydrate diets
     c)   Low protein diets
  3. Point system diet
     a)   Use for losing weight
     b)   Use for gaining weight
  4. Exercise as an element of weight control
     a)   Exercise to help lose weight
     b)   Exercise to help gain weight

Day 17:   Psychological Factors of Fitness
  1. Sound body—sound mind
  2. Positive effects of exercise on mental functioning
     a)   Relief from tension and anxiety
     b)   Build self-confidence
     c)   Build self-discipline
  3. Motivation

Day 18:   Effects of Exercise
  1. General benefits of exercise
  2. Effects of exercise on body systems
     a)   Cardiovascular
     b)   Respiratory
     c)   Skeletal and muscular
     d)   Digestive

e) Endocrine
3. Improved coordination through exercise
4. Increased general activity through exercise

Day 19:   General Conditioning Principles
1. Basic principles for conditioning
  a) Use
  b) Time
  c) Regularity
  d) Adaption
  e) Overload
  f) Progression
2. Conditioning stages
  a) Toughening stage
  b) Slow improvement stage
  c) Challenge stage
3. Cautions
  a) Pushing too far
  b) Drops in fitness level
  c) Warm-up and taper-off

Day 20:   Conditioning Program
1. Isotonic exercise programs
  a) Fitness areas
  b) Sets and repetitions
2. Isometric exercise programs
  a) Fitness areas
  b) Shortcomings
3. Weight training exercise program
  a) Fitness areas
  b) Building muscle size
  c) Increasing muscle firmness

Day 21:   Interrelationship of Fitness Factors
1. Fitness factors cannot be separated—relationships of
  a) Rest
  b) Hygiene
  c) Diet
  d) Exercise
2. Body systems and fitness

Day 22:   Developing Your Own Fitness Program
1. Present program
  a) Conditioning exercises
  b) Isometric exercises
  c) Aerobic routines

2. Criteria for developing a fitness program
    a) Effectiveness
    b) Meeting fitness needs
    c) Enjoyable
3. Practical aspects of individual programs
    a) Selecting a time
    b) Increasing the amount of exercise
    c) Keeping up with program

Day 23:   Last Day
1. Review of weight control
2. Review of personal hygiene
3. Review of rest requirements

Illustrative Lectures

Day 8:   Respiratory system   Today's lesson will be on the respiratory system. First, let's answer the question "What is the respiratory system?" Very simply, the respiratory system takes air into the lungs. The lungs take oxygen from the air and put the oxygen into the blood stream. At the same time, waste products, mostly carbon dioxide, are picked up from the blood and are expelled by the lungs. It is really a marvelous system that can take oxygen from the air, put it into the blood, and at the same time take used-up oxygen, or carbon dioxide, from the blood and breath it back out. All the cells in our body must have oxygen in order to survive. The lungs supply this oxygen. If we do not get enough oxygen in our system, our energy is reduced and our health suffers. You can see how it is important for the lungs to be efficient in taking in oxygen and expelling waste.

There are several diseases that affect the respiratory system. Some of these are emphysema, tuberculosis, asthma, bronchitis, and lung cancer. All of these diseases are influenced by cigarette smoking. In fact, the effects of smoking on the respiratory system are about the same as the effects of the diseases. These diseases clog the lungs, making it harder to breathe.

Smoking does the same thing. Smoking causes shortness of breath, meaning you can take in and breath out less air, just as in some of the diseases. It can damage and destroy lung tissue, reducing the richness and amount of oxygen in the blood. It makes the small veins in your heart and the rest of your body smaller. This slows down the blood circulation. It irritates the lungs. Did you ever get smoke in your eye and feel how it burns? Something very similar to this goes on in the lungs every time you breathe smoke into your lungs. Smoking puts poison into your blood stream, poisons like tar, nicotine, and carbon monoxide. Smoking also increases your chances of heart disease by putting extra strain on the heart by narrowing the blood vessels and reducing the amount of oxygen that is going to the heart muscle. In summary, smoking is the greatest single habit which decreases and retards lung functioning or respiratory functioning. The importance of quitting or cutting down on smoking must be emphasized. It is not easy to quit smoking or even to cut down, but if you will remember that smoking decreases the efficiency of your lungs and your fitness by its negative effect on the lungs and respiratory system, you will see that smoking needs to be curtailed.

There are several ways to stop smoking. Some of them may be good for one individual, others for another. Some of these are worth mentioning. One way is cold turkey, just stop smoking. Another is cutting down gradually over a period of several weeks. Some people have had good luck smoking only half a cigarette; others try using substitutes for smoking, like chewing gum or candy. Exercise can help you stop smoking. If you are breathing heavily from exercise, getting good clean air into your lungs, somehow you don't desire to smoke. Besides helping you quit smoking, exercise is the one way to increase lung or respiratory functioning. Page 11 in your workbook has some suggestions that may help you quit smoking.

Many exercises for respiratory endurance are similar to cardiovascular endurance exercises. The same type and quantity of exercise helps both areas. Running and walking conditions your lungs as well as your heart. Sustained exercise is a key for overcoming many lung diseases.

Let's look at what exercise does for your respiratory system. Exercise increases the amount of oxygen you take in, and the amount of carbon dioxide expelled. In other words, exercise increases the amount of air that is going into your lungs, and many doctors say it improves the ability of your lungs to take in oxygen. It provides what you might call richer blood, in that the blood has more oxygen in it. This makes breathing easier. The exercises we are doing force your body to perform at a higher level over a sustained period of time. Your body uses a lot of oxygen this way, but not enough so your body craves oxygen and you must stop exercising. This is called Aerobic 1 exercise, that is, you are using a lot of oxygen. Aerobic exercises, those exercises done just below the level where your body craves oxygen and you must stop, train your heart and lungs to increase the blood supply to the muscles and other body systems. Your progressive training program is designed to gradually force your body to increase its oxygen intake and increase your circulation. As a result your body performance will increase. All of these will lead to better health.

Day 17: Psychological factors of fitness   Today we are going to talk about psychological factors of fitness. I'll bet you have all heard the old quotation "Sound body, sound mind." This is not just a cliche. This is a fact. There is a strong relationship between physical fitness and mental health. If you increase one, it helps to increase the other. Increased fitness has been shown to be closely related to improved academic and school performance. In short, fitness not only increases your physical functioning but your overall functioning as well, including academic or school performance and your overall mental health. Am I saying that exercise will make you smarter? Not exactly, but since you feel better because of exercise, your mental performance will probably be better too.

Vigorous exercise not only increases your fitness but has positive effects on your emotional and psychological functioning. It can help you relax from tension and anxiety and can help you increase your psychological endurance to undergo psychological stress, just as it helps you undergo physical stress. Increasing fitness is an experience that can give you more self-confidence, more self-respect and pride. Being active and working hard toward fitness is not easy, but it can help you be more self-disciplined and can help you be more action-oriented toward your life. It discourages the tendency to sit back and wait for things to happen to you. It can help you take an honest look at yourself physically. All of these effects have been proven through research, and they can help you fulfill your potentials.

A big factor affecting your starting and carrying out a physical program is your motivation. Motivation means simply why we do things. We like to do things if we are rewarded for them. If we get something we want or if something makes us feel good, that is a reward. I imagine for a lot of you, as for a lot of other people, physical exercise and activity has been a punishment in the past. There was no reward for your effort. The result of this is that most people are not motivated to do physical activities.

The beneficial results of exercise are well worth the effort you must put out. Next time we will discuss the effects of exercise.

RESEARCH REVIEW

This section presents summaries of two studies that were conducted by the authors for the purpose of evaluating the benefits of systematic physical fitness training on clients in a comprehensive rehabilitation center. The summaries are followed by a brief review and discussion of evidence concerning the relationship between fitness and personal adjustment.

The PIE Experimental Study

The first research evaluation of the PF package was conducted in conjunction with an experimental investigation of Carkhuff's PIE (physical, intellectual, emotional) training program, as a treatment mode to improve the rehabilitation potential of disabled clients at the Hot Springs Rehabilitation Center (Roessler, Bolton, Means, and Milligan, 1975). In addition to the PF package, clients in the experimental group received 16 hours of goal setting training (intellectual component) and 16 hours of interpersonal skills training (emotional component).

A randomized experimental/control design utilizing pretest and posttest measures of physical fitness, goal setting, interpersonal skills, self-concept, internal control, and personal adjustment was carried out for 97 subjects. The research sample was composed of younger clients of average intelligence, with more than one half being physically disabled. The specific results of the study were as follows:

1. Experimental clients gained significantly in physical fitness—cardiovascular functioning, flexibility, endurance, and dynamic strength.
2. Interpersonal skills training resulted in significant gains in communication abilities for experimental clients.
3. Goal setting training produced significant improvement in the experimental clients' abilities to set and define goals.
4. No improvement in self-concept as measured by the Tennessee Self-Concept Scale was found.
5. Experimental males tended to improve in their sense of personal control more than did control males; no improvement occurred for experimental females.
6. Experimental females tended to improve on behavior ratings, whereas, control females did not; no differences were found in behavior ratings for males.
7. Center outcomes (completed, dropout, disciplinary dismissal, etc.) were comparable in all groups.

In summary, the statistical results were partially supportive of the tentative conclusion that the PIE program produces improvements in specific physical, goal setting, and interpersonal skills, but that these effects may not generalize immediately to self-concept, internal control, and personal adjustment.

The PF Package Evaluation

The final evaluation of the PF package was carried out using a sample of 20 regular clients at the Hot Springs Rehabilitation Center (Bolton and Milligan, 1976). The research sample consisted of young males with the following major disabilities: behavioral disability (7), mental retardation (4), and physical disability (9). The subjects were divided into two groups that met in consecutive one-hour sessions three days per week for eight weeks.

The effects of the PF package were assessed using three types of measures: 1) physical fitness tests, 2) personal adjustment inventories, and 3) a survey of exercise habits. The first two sets of measures were administered on a pretest/posttest basis while the survey of exercise habits was administered as a posttest only, two months after the program terminated.

The results of the evaluation are summarized as follows:

1. The eight-week PF program produced highly significant im-

provements in all areas of fitness: the largest gains were realized in the areas of dynamic strength and endurance, with substantial improvement in cardiovascular functioning and flexibility. The magnitude of the stability coefficients suggested that all subjects benefited from the program.

2. The PF program resulted in measurable "carry-over" effects, as reflected in responses to the Exercise Habits Questionnaire: the majority of the subjects felt they benefitted from PF, recommended it for other clients, and continued to exercise after the training program was terminated. The most impressive statistics document the change in exercise habits: only two of 14 respondents exercised regularly before the program—afterwards 11 exercised three days per week or more.

3. The PF program did not produce any improvement in self-reported personal adjustment, as measured by the Tennessee Self-Concept Scale and the Mini-Mult. However, the instability of the scales from pretest to posttest rendered the interpretation of the measures questionable.

Physical Fitness and Personal Adjustment

As the results of the two studies summarized above indicate, the effects of the PF program on self-reported personal adjustment are difficult to measure. However, previous research is equivocal regarding the relationship between physical fitness and personal adjustment, expecially self-concept. For example, Christian (1969) investigated the relationship between improved fitness as the result of a six-week training program and change in self-concept for male college students: there was none. Yet, Collingwood and Willett (1971) documented significant increases in physical fitness performance, positive body attitude, positive self-attitude, self-acceptance, and significant decreases in real versus ideal self discrepancy for five obese male teenagers who participated in a three-week physical training program. And Rothfarb (1970) found that college men who exercise or participate regularly in athletics have more positive self-concepts than those who do not. Fitts (1972b) reviewed seven investigations conducted with college age, or younger, subjects and concluded that they "do not show very dramatic relationships between physical fitness and self concept" (p. 35). He commented that "It seems likely that physical health and fitness might be more critical influences on the self concept, or vice versa, in adult populations but this remains to be determined" (Fitts, 1972b, p. 35).

Several factors may explain the lack of consistent relationships between physical fitness and improvement in personal adjustment in the various studies. First, the human personality is a relatively stable entity and is resistant to change, except under the most traumatic circumstances. Second, inventories and questionnaires that purport to measure various aspects of personality functioning and personal adjustment have been designed for optimal reliability and stability, and thus are biased against the detection of change. Third, the pretest/posttest intervals in most studies have not been long enough to allow the PF participants to consolidate and incorporate their fitness gains into their views of themselves. Finally, changes in personal adjustment may depend upon opportunities for the clients to apply newly learned skills and concepts to real life problems beyond the confines of the rehabilitation program. In conclusion, after considering a broad range of empirical evidence and subjective experience, it is our opinion that physical fitness training programs do serve to enhance the personal adjustment and ultimate success of most rehabilitation clients.

SUMMARY

Physical Fitness Training (PF) is an essential component of a comprehensive personal adjustment program. Ten specific benefits that derive from participation in PF activities are: pleasure, enthusiasm, safe reality testing, accomplishment, ego involvement, skill acquisition, socialization, self-expression, self-esteem, and constructive use of leisure time. The PF package consists of three components: an instructor's manual, a participant's manual, and a series of 23 lectures on health and fitness topics. The PF program begins and ends with a fitness evaluation using five standard measures. Each of the 23 classes that are detailed in the PF package consists of two parts: a series of progressive exercises and a brief lecture on a health-related topic. The effectiveness of the PF package in improving the physical condition of rehabilitation clients was documented in two research studies carried out at the Hot Springs Rehabilitation Center. While the results of investigations that have examined the relationship between physical fitness and personality change are equivocal, due primarily to limitations in research design and measurement procedures, there is ample reason to believe that PF improves the personal adjustment of many rehabilitation clients.

Chapter 8

Behavioral Analysis Training

To function effectively as personal adjustment trainers, rehabilitation professionals must thoroughly understand the theory, model, and strategies underlying their view of personal adjustment. One way to view personal adjustment is through the behaviorally oriented approach of Behavioral Analysis Training (Roessler, Means, and Farley, 1977). The main objective of Behavioral Analysis Training (BAT) is to help clients behave more effectively in real life situations. Effectiveness of behavior is defined from the point of view of both client and counselor, based on the short-term and long-term results of the response.

BAT's emphasis on effective behavior stems from the fact that clients are labeled poorly adjusted because others observe them exhibiting ineffective or unusual behaviors. The labels "poorly adjusted" or "maladjusted" are then indiscriminately applied, clustering very different problems together. For example, clients may be too aggressive, too shy, too open, too defensive, or too withdrawn. They may respond inadequately to certain significant situations; e.g., meeting people, taking tests, holding and doing a job, responding to authority, or dealing with family.

BAT emphasizes a more individualized approach to personal adjustment training for rehabilitation. A more personal approach to adjustment problems provides techniques whereby the client and counselor together identify problem situations and ineffective behaviors. They then develop strategies for more effective behaviors in the client's problem areas.

The client's adjustment problem usually is either too much of an inappropriate behavior or too little of an appropriate behavior (Holland, 1970). With facilitation from the counselor, the client can see that he/she is doing something too much (making critical comments) or something too little (making reinforcing comments). The counselor's responsibility is to elicit and clarify the client's feelings and insights regarding himself/herself and, if the insights seem appropriate, help the client understand how to respond more effectively in problematic situations. Because assumptions about personal adjustment are made by observing behavior in specific situations, it follows that the client's behavior changes, if appropriate, would cause others to infer that the client is, in fact, becoming better adjusted.

UNDERSTANDING PERSONAL ADJUSTMENT

Understanding personal adjustment and how to develop it, then, begins by deciding whether it is a trait or general condition that a person possesses, or a concept relative to "behavior in situation." BAT's point of view is that adjustment is a situationally specific concept, i.e., individuals are adjusted or effective in some situations and not in others. In other words, one person may respond effectively in meeting job responsibilities but ineffectively in dealing with marital problems. For another individual, the reverse may be true.

Judging from observations of behavior, adjustment is situation specific; it is relative to the behavior exhibited in a particular situation. The behavior reflects what the person has learned and been rewarded for over a period of time in similar situations. If the behavior is effective, that is, neither creating nor increasing a problem but in some way solving one, the person is judged to be well adjusted. On the other hand, should the person respond ineffectively in another situation, that is, creating or increasing a problem, the individual would be judged maladjusted.

In short, BAT's importance is that it does not assume that adjustment is a personal trait that a person either has or does not have. Rather, adjustment is reflected in what the person has learned to do in a number of different situations. Hence, to increase personal adjustment, a counselor needs basically to help a client learn to respond effectively in situations previously characterized by inappropriate responses and feelings of dissatisfaction and, in this way, to shed the general label of being maladjusted.

In BAT, enhancing personal adjustment means increasing effective responses to life situations. The client and counselor, working together, set behavioral goals representing effective resolution of problem situations. First, client and counselor identify situations in which the client feels he/she is responding inadequately. Next, they discuss the client's perceptions of self in those situations. Is the client responding with too much or too little of a given behavior? What could he/she do to respond appropriately in the situation?

In terms of developing effective responses, BAT covers a number of approaches to behavior change. At a very general level, behavior change can come about through modifying the situation or through modifying the person's responses to that situation. Presumably, changing the situation will cause the person to respond differently. If it is impossible to change the situation, the person must learn new behaviors for responding to that persistent situation. In either case, changing the situation or changing the responses, the client will be judged adjusted or maladjusted depending upon manifest behavioral responses (Skinner, 1966).

Because clients vary in their ability to respond effectively in different situations, the counselor must have a system for dealing with a variety of adjustment (behavioral) goals. Some clients may behave adequately on the job but not in the family. Some may be overly assertive, while others may be withdrawn and submissive. Hence, the counselor will have not only different goals for different clients, but different strategies to help these clients reach their goals. Application of the BAT exercises results in the development of personal adjustment strategies individually tailored to the needs of each client so that he/she can learn to respond more effectively to particular problem situations in life (Krumboltz, 1966).

Different Goals/Different Strategies

To some, the concept of different goals and different strategies may imply that there is no commonality in Behavioral Analysis Training. However, BAT is based on a set of assumptions central to a "behavior in situation" approach to personal adjustment:

1. A "behavior in situation" approach has as its objective the enhancement of personal adjustment by helping clients learn to respond more effectively to problematic situations.
2. Problem situations may differ from client to client.
3. Strategies for responding more effectively to problem situations may differ from client to client.
4. Regardless of their nature, client goals must eventually be expressed in behavioral terms.
5. Clients must know why their goals are important and how to achieve them.
6. The chief training emphasis is on replacing the present association of ineffective behaviors in a given situation with a new association between that same situation and effective behavioral responses.

In short, clients can better understand their needs by seeing them defined in terms of behavioral goals and effective responses in problematic situations. Though such behavioral analysis fosters client readiness to change, it does not ensure it. Only when clients recognize the potential value of changing will they be ready to cooperate in a personal adjustment training program.

Readiness for Behavioral Analysis Training

Various factors operate singly or in combination to make an individual ready for Behavioral Analysis Training. Generally speaking, the individual may feel that responding differently in a problem situation will create access to reinforcements that are not presently available. On the other hand, the person may feel that responding differently in a given situation will help him/her avoid real or threatened punishment. Gaining reinforcement or avoiding punishment, then, are general reasons for self-control of behavior change (readiness).

More specifically, initiation of self-control may result from one of the following:

1. Threatened retaliation from social agencies
2. Availability of new information
3. Feedback from friends and social acquaintances
4. Internal experiences, e.g., guilt, embarrassment, or shame (Goldfried and Merbaum, 1973, p. 12)
5. Recognition of growth or self-development potential of the new behaviors (Kolb and Boyatzis, 1970; Kolb, Winter, and Berlew, 1968)

Additional features pertinent to the client's personal orientation in the goal-setting experience also affect the outcome of self-control efforts. For example, Kolb and Boyatzis (1970) demonstrated the validity of the following hypotheses:

1. Individuals will change more on those dimensions of their self-concepts that they define as relevant to their consciously set change goal than they will on dimensions of their self-concepts that they define as not relevant. This change will be independent of the difficulty of the change goal (p. 441).
2. Individuals who are successful in achieving their change goals will initially show a greater awareness of forces related to those change goals than will individuals who are unsuccessful in achieving their change goals (p. 442).

3. Individuals who are successful in achieving their change goals will show ... more indications that they expect success than will individuals who are not successful in achieving their goals (p. 442).
4. Individuals who are successful in achieving their change goals will indicate greater psychological safety during the goal-setting process than will individuals who are not successful (p. 443).
5. Individuals who are successful in achieving their change goals will be more likely to give consideration to measuring progress toward their goals than those who are not successful (p. 443).
6. Individuals who are successful in achieving their change goals will be more likely to feel that the control of reinforcement that they receive during the change process rests with themselves than will those who are not successful (p. 444).

Interpretation of the Kolb and Boyatzis (1970) data follows two lines of logic. Initially, their findings help the counselor identify clients who are likely to do well or poorly in a self-change effort. In addition, their findings also suggest the need for various techniques, such as "supportiveness, collaborative goal-setting, emphasis on self-direction, behavior monitoring and control, and selective reinforcement," that the counselor can use to increase the probability that clients will accomplish their goals.

Even though the client may be ready to accomplish a certain goal, the counselor must determine whether or not the goal is an appropriate adjustment objective; this decision requires criteria for personal adjustment goals. Krumboltz (1966) suggested the following criteria for counseling goals:

1. Counseling goals should be capable of being stated differently for each individual client.
2. Counseling goals, for each client, should be compatible with, though not necessarily identical to, the values of his/her counselor.
3. The degree to which the goals of counseling are attained by each client should be observable (pp. 154–155).

Behavioral Analysis Training follows the principles presented by Krumboltz; different clients will have different goals. In Behavioral Analysis Training, counselors should feel comfortable working with certain goals in terms of their values and skills. Finally, BAT stresses that client goals be behaviorally defined, observable, and capable of measurement.

Behavior Change Strategies

One of the chief strategies of BAT is an aspect of operant conditioning labeled self-controlled behavior change. Self-controlled behavior change involves the client in a functional analysis of personal behavior. The functional analysis helps clients determine what they are doing in different situations and what they would like to do in those same situations to be more personally effective. Actual self-control of behavior begins only when the client is ready to respond in new ways to problematic situations and knows how to do so.

Very simply, a behavior change strategy involves learning and giving new responses to problematic situations. A term related to behavior change strategies, reflective of the effort of learning new responses, is "program development." Program development, an approach to behavior change, focuses on identifying and specifying effective behaviors in problem situations.

Program Development

Program development involves building new responses to situations that have in the past elicited ineffective responses. One of the principals of BAT is that clients themselves be involved in the process of programming. In one sense, clients become their own counselors by evaluating what they are doing and deciding what they want to do. At the same time, they use outside resources in the form of their counselor and the training and skills that the counselor can bring to bear on the problem.

BEHAVIORAL ANALYSIS TRAINING

Behavioral Analysis Training emphasizes two activities: identifying a behavioral goal and specifying performances required to reach that goal. The steps required to identify a goal and its component behaviors have been outlined in a number of resources (Armstrong and Bakker, 1976; Cautela, 1968; Gambrill, Thomas and Carter, 1971; Holland, 1970; Lawrence and Sundel, 1972; Thomas and Walter, 1973). In Behavioral Analysis Training, techniques are provided to complete the following phases:

1. Problem identification—What are the personal adjustment problems impairing the client's vocational and social success?
2. Problem definition—What are the situations that elicit problem behaviors and the consequences of problem behaviors involved in the client's current difficulties?

3. Readiness to change—Has the client reached a point where change is sincerely desired? Can the client carry out self-change efforts? Who else might help the client maintain a behavior change program?
4. Resolution behaviors—How many alternative ways exist to resolve the problem? What are the behaviors involved in realizing the most desirable alternative? What reinforcers might support client change efforts?
5. Incentives—What does the client enjoy, desire, etc., that could be made contingent upon following the new behavioral approach?
6. Programming—What are the specific behavioral steps for resolving the problems? What rewards are contingent upon following each step? How can steps and rewards be contracted for by the client?
7. Monitoring—How can the client analyze progress on the behavioral program? What steps exist to maintain behavior change?
8. Termination—What other problem areas might be dealt with through Behavior Analysis Training? Has the client learned the skills well enough to generalize them to other situations?

Problem Identification

Programming begins by identifying an area of dissatisfaction in the client's life. Several approaches exist to identify areas of dissatisfaction. One approach is to introduce categories of problem situations, for example, studying, dating, etc., for the client to consider in terms of his/her personal problems (D'Zurilla and Goldfried, 1971). A related approach used in BAT is a problem-oriented interview based on the Mooney Problem Check List (Mooney and Gordon, 1950). Clients explore the following areas to identify problems of potential significance: health and physical development; finances, living conditions, and employment; social and recreational activities; relationships with other people outside the family; and home and family.

Additional self-report approaches to problem identification are suggested. Clients could complete an adapted value clarification exercise, the Five Things list (Simon, Howe, and Kirschenbaum, 1972), an adapted adjective checklist (LaForge and Suczek, 1955), or Cantril's (1965) Self-anchoring Life Ladder. Instructions are provided in the BAT manual for translating the self-report data into meaningful client problem statements.

A method for integrating an outside perspective on client problems, Patient and Progress Evaluation Recording (PAPER) (Biostatistics Unit, 1972), is also introduced in the manual. Although the PAPER system is most appropriate for a facility setting, it provides a way for other staff familiar with the client to specify adjustment problems they have observed in the client's behavior. Staff input is then incorporated in the analysis for counselor and client to discuss during the problem identification phase.

During the problem identification or orientation (D'Zurilla and Goldfried, 1971) phase, counselor and client focus on the problem or problems discussed by the client. Generally, the counselor should ask the client to provide background to the problems and to describe how he/she feels about himself/herself in these problem situations. Often clients will describe themselves in negative terms and advance some reasons for why they would like to change. The negative trait or traits the person attributes to himself/herself represent the beginning points of Behavioral Analysis Training.

For example, clients may say that they behave too much one way and too little another way, e.g., they may feel that they are too assertive or not assertive enough. They may feel that they are too impulsive or not impulsive enough. In essence, clients are really saying that they would like to respond more effectively to problem situations so that they can attribute more positive traits to themselves.

In discussing the client's self-image and troublesome situations, the counselor gets a feeling for problem areas in the client's life. Counselor and client may decide to focus on one or several of these problem areas or situations in detail. The next phase, problem definition, demonstrates how the selected problems can be clarified in a functional sense.

Problem Definition

After identifying a problem area in the client's self-image, the next step is to identify the situation in which the client feels that he/she is responding ineffectively. In behavioral terminology, the counselor and the client are now looking at the client's life in terms of stimulus control. Stimulus control simply means that a situation or set of stimuli are associated with certain reactions on the client's part. For the purpose of BAT, the client's reaction to the problem should reflect a personal desire to change.

At this point, counselor and client must define very specifically where and when the client does what he/she now wants to change. In other words, in what situation does the client respond in ways that lead to negative self-evaluations?

After identifying the problem situation, the client and the counselor should determine the responses that the client is currently giving in that situation. The set of responses represents a chain of behavior which client and counselor clarify by completing the following sentence stems:

1. I am dissatisfied because I am _____ (describe yourself)
2. I am this way when _____ (describe situation)
3. When I am in that situation, I act this way first _____ (describe your behavior)
4. Then the other person responds this way _____ (describe other's behavior)
5. Then I act this way _____ (describe your behavior)
6. Then I feel this way _____ (describe your feeling)
7. Sometimes I do these things to _____ (describe other related behaviors)

Another activity complementing the behavior analysis is the reinforcement sheet developed by D'Zurilla and Goldfried (1971). In completing the reinforcement sheet, clients examine the personal and social consequences of their behavior from both a short-term and a long-term perspective. Responses to the activity identify the reinforcers maintaining the behaviors and clarify the fact that the behaviors, although leading to short-term rewards, eventually result in long-term negative consequences.

The client, with the counselor's help, should fill in each of the categories of the reinforcement exercise, personal short- and long-term consequences and social short- and long-term consequences. Then each must focus on the question, "Is the client ready to develop new behaviors that lead to positive consequences and avoid the negative consequences of what he/she is presently doing?"

Readiness For Change

Even though clients may feel ready to accomplish a certain goal, the counselor must also determine whether or not the goal is realistic for the client. Hence, the readiness phase involves determining both whether or not the client finds the current situation aversive enough to stimulate behavior change efforts, and whether or not the potential change efforts are realistic given client and/or situational limitations.

Schwartz and Goldiamond (1975, p. 80) provide an extremely workable structured interview approach for assessing client readiness. Initial questions deal with why the client wants to change now. The client's assets for making a change are then evaluated in the following categories:

Related skills—What skills or strengths do you have which are related to what you would like to do?

Other skills—What others do you have?

Stimulus control—Are there conditions when the present problem is not a problem?

Relevant problem solving repertoire—In the past, what related problems did you tackle successfully? How?

Other problems solved—What other problems did you tackle successfully? How?

Past control—Did you once have mastery of the present problem area? If so, when and under what circumstances? Any idea of how?

Client and counselor also review data from the reinforcement sheet to determine whether or not the client is receiving any special benefits from the current problem behaviors. Finally, the client is asked to list ways in which others (family, friends, etc.) can assist in the behavior change process.

A more detailed approach to examining client readiness was developed by Kanfer and Saslow (1965, 1968). Their material is concerned with the wide variety of organism, person, and environmental factors placing limits on the client. The counselor would do well to review the following issues to determine whether it is appropriate to move to the resolution behavior phase:

Developmental Analysis

1. What are the limitations of the client's biological equipment that may affect current behavior?

2. How do these limitations initiate or maintain undesirable behavior?

3. Can the client's self-limiting expectations of the interfering consequences be changed? How?

4. When and how did biological deviations or limitations develop? What consequences did they have for the client's life pattern or self-attitudes? What was done by whom? Has the client developed consistent response patterns toward some body structure or function?

5. How do these biological conditions limit response to treatment or resolution of the problem?

Social Changes

1. What are the most characteristic features of the client's present sociocultural milieu, e.g., rural, urban, religious affiliation, economic status, ethnic affiliation, and education/intellectual affiliation?

2. Will the proposed behavior changes bring the client into conflict with the sociocultural milieu (the client's immediate social environment)?

3. Have there been changes in the client's environment that are pertinent to his/her current behavior? If so, how long ago, how permanently? What immediate and long range consequences did these changes have? What attitudes does the client have about these changes?

4. Are the client's roles in the various social settings congruent with one another? Does the problematic behavior occur in all or only some of the different settings?

5. How can identified sociological factors in the problematic behavior be brought into relationship with the treatment program?

Analysis of Self-Control

1. In what situations can the client control the behaviors that are problematic? How does he/she achieve such control (by manipulation of self and/or others)?

2. Have any of the problem behaviors been followed by aversive consequences by others, e.g., social retribution, ostracism, probation? Have these conditions reduced the frequency of the problem behavior or only the condition under which it occurs? Have these events modified the client's self-controlling behavior?

3. Has the client acquired some measure of self-control in avoiding situations that are conducive to execution of the problematic behavior? Does he/she do this by avoidance or substitution of altered instrumental behaviors leading to similar satisfaction?

4. Is there correspondence between the client's verbalized degree of self-control and observations by others? Can the client match behavior to intentions?

5. What conditions, persons, or reinforcers tend to change self-controlling behaviors?

6. To what extent can the client's self-control be used in a treat-
    ment program? Is constant supervision needed?

Analysis of Social Relationships

1. Who are the most significant people in the client's current
    environment? Who facilitates constructive behavior and who
    provokes problematic behaviors?
2. How can the people who influence the client positively par-
    ticipate in treatment? (Adapted from Kanfer and Saslow, 1968)

Resolution Behaviors

As problem situations and goals are clarified, the counselor must
examine the goals in terms of certain decision-making criteria. Is the
client ready to work on the goal? Does the counselor feel comfortable with the goal? Is it a goal area in which the counselor has
or can attain some competencies? Is it a goal that is observable
and, to some degree, measurable?

If the goal is an appropriate one for the behavior resolution
phase, the counselor can begin by reinforcing the client's basic sense
of internal control. In other words, the counselor needs to reinforce
the client's feeling that he/she has the personal resources, although
he/she may not yet know exactly how to use them to deal successfully with the problem (Kolb and Boyatzis, 1970).

In the resolution behaviors phase, the counselor using Behavioral Analysis Training would help the client develop more effective forms of behaviors leading to positive short- and long-term
consequences. With the help of the counselor, the client can develop
a new chain of behaviors aimed at lessening or eliminating current
problems. Thinking positively, both counselor and client state what
the client must do to feel satisfied. How would the client like to see
himself/herself? In what situation would he/she like to be that way?
What would he/she have to do in that situation to feel worthy of a
more positive self-description? Again, incomplete sentence stems are
used to encourage exploration of resolution behaviors.

1. I would be satisfied if I were _____ (describe yourself)
2. I want to act differently when _____ (restate problem situation)
3. When I am in that situation, I would like to act this way _____
    (describe desired behaviors)
4. The other person would probably act this way _____ (describe
    other's behavior)
5. Then I would _____ (describe desired behavior)

6. Then I would feel this way _____ (describe your feeling)
7. Here are some other things I want to do _____ (describe desired behaviors)

Two other exercises are provided to encourage brainstorming of resolution behaviors, a "Ways" sheet and a "Satisfaction Behavior" sheet. On the Ways sheet, the client lists all possible ways to accomplish the goal. Because the emphasis is on imagination and creativity, no effort is made to screen or censor any ideas. Having completed the Ways exercise, the client evaluates the probability of each behavioral possiblity leading to goal attainment. The more feasible steps for each goal are then listed in the order they should be taken on the Satisfaction Behavior Identification sheet.

After completing the resolution behavior activities, the client should consider consequences of the new behaviors. Will these new behaviors be reinforcing for the client? Is the client ready to follow these behaviors in order to gain rewards or to avoid punishment? Methods for encouraging client goal-oriented behavior are discussed in the incentives section.

Incentives

Behavior change programs developed through Behavior Analysis Training have many built-in incentives for following program steps. For example, clients receive positive feedback from others as they modify problem behaviors. Concurrently, they experience a feeling of accomplishment as they actually follow the steps of their program.

It may be advisable to buttress these built-in incentives with additional short-term rewards administered by the client (Watson and Tharp, 1972). These short-term rewards can be made contingent upon following the steps of the behavioral program. For example, by completing step one on a certain date, the client could obtain a reward such as dinner at a favorite restaurant, a show, or one hour for a favorite recreation. However, there are two important considerations in self-administering reinforcers for following behavioral steps. First, clients must identify the reinforcers they desire; self-selection of rewards increases the probability that the client will actually work for them. Second, the client must adhere to previously worked out schedules of reinforcement. In other words, the behavioral step must be completed before the reward is taken. Some clients will benefit from counselor monitoring at this point.

The steps for selecting reinforcers for behavioral programs include the identification of personal incentives, ranking of incentives, and the pairing of incentives with behavioral steps. During the incentive phase, the client selects personal reinforcers by responding to a questionnaire developed by Watson and Tharp (1972). These reinforcers are then rank ordered in terms of desirability in preparation for completing the behavioral contract during the program development phase.

In addition, a second reinforcement sheet should be prepared to demonstrate that the client can expect both short- and long-term positive consequences from the new behaviors. All four categories of the sheet (personal/social, short/long-term) should be completed based on the individual's perception of what is to be gained by adopting a new set of behaviors. Because the client will not attempt to change during the program development phase if the rewards are insufficient, the counselor must be certain that the client is satisfied with the contingencies or rewards available.

Programming

After completing the Behavior Analysis forms (dissatisfaction and satisfaction), the Ways sheet, the Satisfaction Behaviors sheet, and the two reinforcement sheets, client and counselor are ready to pull together client data into a step-by-step behavioral adjustment program. One format for behavioral programming is the Program Development Sheet, which parallels the individualized written rehabilitation program forms developed by state vocational rehabilitation agencies. Sections of the program development form include: goal statement, behavioral steps, rewards for completing steps, deadlines, and results of each step. Data pertinent to the goal definition and behavioral steps can be obtained from previously completed materials. Counselor and client should then establish deadlines for the accomplishment of each step.

In setting the stage for program development, counselor and client should again discuss the way in which the client would like to see himself/herself; for example, more assertive, more open, more honest, etc. Then, they should discuss the situation where the target behavior is appropriate. The situation will be the original problematic situation discussed at the beginning of the functional analysis of behavior.

Program development involves a creative recombination of behaviors from exercises, discussions, etc. into a new chain of behavioral steps that lead to satisfaction. The step-by-step approach is based on principles of successive approximation. The first step the client takes is one that he/she is already doing; subsequent steps are increasingly difficult, but only in small degrees.

Often the first step in a program is one called "stop and think" (Skinner, 1953). It requires that the client stop and think about a situation—in a sense talk to himself/herself to delay impulsive or habitual behavior in that situation—and then implement the new behavior program. The "stop and think" step merely says that the client should first analyze the situation as to whether or not it is the problematic situation. If it is, it is now appropriate to implement the more effective behavioral steps.

In program development, the counselor may need outside consultation from other counselors, vocational trainers, psychological resources, etc. The counselor can use outside resources, exercises completed by the client, and insights from discussions with the client to develop an effective behavioral program.

After client and counselor have completed the program development sheet, the client should then write the steps from the program on a contract sheet and sign the contract. The contract sheet re-emphasizes the importance of taking steps in order and of making a public commitment to a goal (Winter, Griffith, and Kolb, 1968). Some clients will want to list on the contract specific reinforcements for each program step. Others may only want to write at the bottom of the contract the personal and social short- and long-term rewards to be gained from the program.

Program development may take many forms. For example, the program may be highly situation specific in the sense that client and counselor develop a new chain of behaviors to respond to a problem situation. Or the program may draw on existing behavioral techniques, e.g., desensitization training, relaxation training, assertiveness training, or other behavior control strategies that are available.

For most programs, the counselor will work directly with the client. In some instances of behavior modification, such as assertiveness training, desensitization training, relaxation training, counterconditioning, etc., the counselor may not feel competent to carry out steps of the program. In such cases, the counselor should acquire outside assistance for the client while at the same time continuing to work with the client in monitoring goal progress.

The final program is based on joint counselor and client decisions drawing on data from discussions of the functional analysis of behavior. When the program is completed, the client is ready to consider ways to monitor progress toward the behavioral goal.

Monitoring

The concept of monitoring goal progress requires further clarification before the client is ready to act on the goal program. One approach to progress monitoring that is particularly useful is goal attainment scaling (Goodyear and Bitter, 1974; Kiresuk, Salasin, and Garwick, 1972). It states that any goal or program effort can lead to one of five possible attainment levels: best possible, better than expected, expected, less than expected, or worst possible.

To use goal attainment scaling in BAT, the counselor and client define the various achievement levels possible through the program they have prepared. Each level should be stated in observable, yet meaningful terms. The client should state his/her present level on the goal somewhere below expected attainment level. For example, if the client feels that conditions could deteriorate—he/she could become even less assertive—then his/her state should be written as a less-than-expected attainment level. If the client feels that the problem could get no worse than it is now, he/she should characterize the present level on the goal as worst possible. The client next marks the intake level, and dates the Goal Attainment Worksheet. Remaining levels, best possible, better than expected, and expected, etc., are completed.

Having completed the functional analysis of behavior and the goal attainment scale, the client is ready to act on the program step by step. Both the client and the counselor monitor progress in the program. The counselor should determine whether or not the client is following the program in the proper sequence, and whether or not the client is administering reinforcement in terms of some earlier agreement.

The client should also be noting the results that he/she is actually having with the program and comparing them with what was anticipated. Furthermore, the client, along with the counselor, should occasionally note current goal attainment level for the client's program. A goal attainment worksheet has been developed which the client completes to initiate periodic monitoring sessions.

During monitoring, problems in the goal program manifest themselves in two ways. First, the client may not be achieving the anticipated results—he/she may be locked into a less-than-expected attainment level. Or, actual results may be in opposition to anticipated results. If progress is not as expected, client and counselor should review the functional analysis of behavior. Program steps may require modification in order to ensure positive movement on the goal attainment scale and, eventually, goal attainment. With the accomplishment of the goal, client and counselor move to the termination phase.

Termination

The goals of the final phase, termination, are threefold: 1) to determine whether or not clients have learned the different Behavior Analysis Training skills, 2) to determine whether or not clients can use the skills, and 3) to identify some additional areas where clients can use Behavior Analysis Training in their own lives. These three goals are accomplished through some simple activities, e.g., the client responds to several questions tapping cognitive understanding of BAT, analyzes a case vignette using BAT skills, and completes an additional Five Things list to identify future areas where BAT techniques could be applied in his/her life.

SUMMARY

The phases of Behavior Analysis Training are: problem identification, problem definition, readiness to change, resolution behaviors, incentives, programming, monitoring, and termination. In completing each of these steps of the problem-solving process, clients move systematically toward goal attainment. In achieving their goals, clients become more personally effective in problematic situations. This effectiveness manifests itself in observable behaviors that enable the person to feel more satisfied about life, and that enable others to conclude that the individual is making gains in personal adjustment. As clients make adjustment gains, they experience greater self-control in their lives. Furthermore, in gaining this self-control, they have learned a series of skills in functional behavior analysis that they can apply to other difficult real life situations. Generalization of the skills to other situations makes it even more likely that clients will continue to grow in terms of personal adjustment. Indeed, the end goal of BAT is that clients become able to use their own resources to behave more effectively in problematic life situations.

Chapter 9

Coordination of Human Services

Improving psychosocial adjustment to severe disability requires a multifaceted service program designed to meet the many needs of the disabled. One such comprehensive and systematic program to assist the spinal cord injured was described in Chapter 4. The rationale of this project was that multiple services must be offered in a coordinated and timely fashion if the considerable physical and psychological effects of spinal cord injury are to be overcome.

The same concept of coordinated service delivery to enhance psychosocial and vocational outcomes of clients with disabilities can be carried over to the field setting. To be maximally effective, coordinated social and rehabilitative services should aim at meeting the needs of both the disabled client and of his or her family. Therefore, this chapter focuses on concepts central to the integration of service delivery to meet the total needs of the client household.

SERVICE COORDINATION AND CLIENT OUTCOMES

Conclusions from theory (Gray, Duhl, and Rizzo, 1969; Hansell, 1969; Spiegel, 1969) and practice (Margolin, 1955; Stotsky, Mason, and Semaras, 1958; Wright, Reagles, and Butler, 1969) support the contention that coordination of the delivery of human services can add to the effectiveness of traditional approaches to service delivery. Generally, this added effectiveness is operationalized in terms of improved outcomes for consumers in emotional, social, physical, family, economic, and vocational statuses. In addition, an integrated services program should lead to greater system efficiency. Efficiency of service delivery encompasses such concepts as ratio of referral to acceptance, time in service, and closure rate.

Integration is a term used to describe efforts employed in coordinating the activities of various human service agencies so that consumers and their households receive a more comprehensive service package with less duplication of agency effort. Present interest in integration results from the recognition that consumer services are often provided in a fragmented manner. Overcoming fragmented approaches to service delivery is increasingly important, because the Department of Health, Education, and Welfare (DHEW) estimates that 86 to 95% of all DHEW clients have multiple problems (Spencer, 1973).

Several alternatives are available for the development of a coordinated and comprehensive method of serving consumers. Functions, responsibilities, authorities, and personnel of existing human service agencies can be merged into a broad "superagency." The formal authority vested in the director of a superagency allows supervisory and service personnel to be compelled to consolidate planning, budgeting, service delivery, and evaluation.

Integration of services can also refer to mediated sharing of common supportive services by agencies that still retain their separate structure and functions. The cooperating agencies may share buildings, maintenance services, clerical services, and general administrative services. In addition, the agencies cooperate closely in the delivery of services so as to ensure that the entire constellation of family and personal needs receive attention.

Recent Research

Recent research underscores the strengths of a "mediated sharing" approach to service coordination. For example, a team approach to delinquent behavior was developed in Tulsa, Oklahoma. One group of young people received a supervised program of individualized instruction and counseling coupled with the coordinated attention of project counselors from the Juvenile Court, the Rehabilitation Department, and the Welfare Department. A matched group of students received no special assistance other than the normal services of the individual agencies. The comparison confirmed the relative superiority of the integrated approach to delinquency. The study concluded that "there is a need for greater flexibility among participating agencies to make an 'adequate' team approach" (Wright, Reagles, and Butler, 1969).

Ericson and Moberg (Wright, Reagles, and Butler, 1969) reported that an integrated services approach to rehabilitation of convicts led to decreased rates of recidivism and to positive changes on outcome and employment indices. The program offered comprehensive social, psychological, and rehabilitation services through a team approach. According to the authors, both the comprehensiveness and the continuity of the services contributed to the project's success.

Another suggestion of the effectiveness of the team approach comes from the findings of the Community Rehabilitation Project (Wright and Trotter, 1968). Three delivery methods were examined: 1) a team recommends a rehabilitation plan and coordinates its implementation by the cooperating agencies, 2) a team recommends a plan that is then implemented by the cooperating agencies, and 3) the client is provided with services according to a standard interagency referral process.

When the appropriateness of the client's vocational goals was considered, improvement was significantly better when the team had both recommended and implemented a rehabilitation plan. Contrary to expectation, the traditional approach was next in effectiveness, exceeding that of the approach in which the team recommended a plan but did not assist in the plan's implementation. The report concluded that vocational success is poorest when a rehabilitation plan is formulated by one group and implemented by another.

Overall, the team approach of the Community Rehabilitation Project enhanced the mutual understanding and cooperation among the agencies and the emphasis on a well-formulated plan for client service and follow-up. According to Wright and Trotter (1968), the project contributed to reduction in rehabilitation costs, achievement of rehabilitation goals, and an increase in agency and interagency efficiency. By utilizing systems concepts, the apparent superiority of this coordinated team approach can be explained in more theoretical terms.

Systems Theory and Integrated Services

Consistent with the interaction model of behavior discussed in Chapter 3, the systems approach emphasizes the influence of a number of factors—biological, psychological, social, and cultural—on human behavior. According to Spiegel (1969), the "corollary" to this proposition about human behavior is that no single human service agency can meet all the needs of the client and his or her household. Research has indicated that mobilization of various systems with the expressed intent of assisting the client can lead to a significant degree of rehabilitation success (Margolin, 1955; Stotsky, Mason, and Semaras, 1958).

Mental health centers such as the H. Douglas Singer Zone Center (Rockford, Illinois) have operationalized this systems concept in their service delivery program (Hansell, 1969). For example, the Zone Center mission is that of serving as a "convener" of the agents or agencies concerned with the client's problems. By bringing these agencies together, the Zone Center facilitates the coalescence of services and agencies into an interrelated system. This coalescence of services creates a series of treatment possibilities not otherwise available. Hence, the approach to behavior change, because of its systematic and comprehensive nature, becomes more effective.

Increasing the Effectiveness of Service Coordination

In recent research pertinent to serving the mentally retarded, Aiken et al. (1972) identified two elements that were crucial to the effectiveness of service coordination. Essentially, these two elements focused on the extent to which client and administrative requirements were met. Obviously, the strength of the client-centered approach is its focus on the needs of the consumer within an integrated system. The weakness of the client-centered focus is its lack of systematic planning of the total service delivery program. The converse is true of the administrative or community organization approach. According to Aiken et al. (1972), neither aspect is superior to the other; an effective service coordination system requires that both needs be met.

Meeting client requirements necessitates that clients be involved in case planning. Such participation has a number of potential benefits (Aiken et al., 1972; Goldin, 1971; Wright, 1960). It increases communication between service providers and the client, which leads to a better understanding on the client's part of the service program. From this better understanding develops a commitment to the plan and increased motivation to achieve the rehabilitation goal (Coch and French, 1948).

Research in industrial psychology supports the expectation of positive effects from participation in goal setting (Bass and Leavitt, 1963; Kahn and Katz, 1953; Katz, Macoby, and Morse, 1950; Lowin, 1968; Wickert, 1951). Of course, if the decision is not central to one's daily life or if it exerts little control over events, participative decision-making is meaningless (Lowin, 1968; Wilson, 1969). Assuming that the individual is participating in a meaningful way, improved performance in an industrial context has been attributed to the following three factors: 1) increased commitment to the plan, 2) increased knowledge regarding the plan, and 3) increased trust in management's intentions (Lake, Ritvo, and O'Brien, 1969). However, as Aiken et al. (1972) pointed out, participation is only one of the client requirements for an effective coordinated system. Another important factor is monitoring or case management.

A number of research studies have underscored the importance of case management to service coordination (Arkansas Rehabilitation Service, 1961; Goldin, 1971; Margolin, 1955; Stotsky, Mason, and Semaras, 1958). This case management involves monitoring client progress throughout the service delivery program. Because new needs may develop, the service program must be administered in a flexible manner by a figure who is "centrally significant to the client" (Goldin, 1971, p. 192). The careful management of a wide variety of services from a number of human service agencies also leads to a more intensive service program for the client. The intensiveness of the service intervention has been found to be directly related to client satisfaction with services (Reagles, Wright, and Butler, 1970).

With this background from the research literature regarding service coordination, the team approach, and client requirements, one has a basis for examining an experimental service coordination project completed recently in Arkansas. The basic premise of the Arkansas study was that service coordination would improve client outcomes, increase agency efficiency, and increase client satisfaction.

A SERVICE COORDINATION PROJECT[1]

In 1972, Arkansas Social and Rehabilitative Services (SRS) received a three-year grant to implement and evaluate a service coordination project. The Project was carried out by Regional Integrated Services (RIS) at the Arkansas Services Center in Jonesboro, a co-located site for seven service agencies (Vocational Rehabilitation, Rehabilitation for the Blind, Mental Health, Mental Retardation, Juvenile Services, Social Services, and Public Health).

Project Design

The Regional Integrated Services Project (Roessler and Mack,

---

[1] This section is adapted from Roessler and Mack (1976), with permission of the copyright holder, the National Rehabilitation Counseling Association.

1975b) featured non-categorical program administration, shared core service functions, shared management information, and research evaluation. The non-categorical program administration was carried out by Social and Rehabilitative Service employees charged with the responsibility of developing and implementing procedures to enhance interagency coordination. Shared core service functions included hiring and training a staff of case managers to assist agencies in developing coordinated service programs. As a support to agency representatives, a shared management information system was developed to provide data regarding household needs and service requirements. The research and evaluation component carried out an ongoing evaluation of the implemented system.

The three approaches to service coordination evaluated in the Project included a traditional approach, a coordinated approach, and a coordinated/case-managed approach. The traditional approach, although not having the additional resources provided at the Arkansas Services Center, included case coordination as an implicit duty of each service representative. During the course of the study, no special mention of or emphasis on the importance of coordinated services was made in the traditional setting. However, some sensitization regarding service coordination may have occurred due to the activity of Arkansas Social and Rehabilitative Services in the neighboring county and throughout the state.

The coordinated group approach emphasized case management but did not require direct contact between client and case manager. A common intake form completed during the initial field agency contact was forwarded to Regional Integrated Services, where case managers screened client household information for additional referrals. Clients were contacted by mail, and agencies by interoffice memo, regarding potential client household referrals. Case managers followed up to see if clients and their household members had responded to the referrals. While the agencies provided services to the clients and their families, the case managers served the client households by monitoring case progress and by communicating new case information to all involved agencies.

Trained in goal setting and interpersonal skills, case managers in the coordinated/case-managed approach helped clients to define personal goals and to understand how the goals could be met through coordinated social and rehabilitative services. Standard procedures and forms were used to identify client and client household problems, to interpret the problems into broad areas of human needs, to translate human needs into agency referrals and potential services, and to identify barriers to receiving services, e.g., transportation, childcare, etc. (Roessler, Mack, and Statler, 1975). Service information was drawn together in a brief plan presented to the client by the case manager. The plan included services responding to client and client household goals and to other needs recognized by the service agencies.

As they monitored client progress, case managers recorded how well clients were achieving their goals. At least two client/case manager contacts were included in the monitoring phase.

Research Results

The research problem called for comparing the effectiveness, efficiency, and responsiveness of the three different approaches to coordinating service delivery—the traditional approach, coordination, and coordination/case management. Due to the additional resources for coordinating services at the Arkansas Services Center, it was hypothesized that effectiveness, efficiency, and responsiveness differences would favor clients assigned to the coordination and coordination/case management groups.

Clients were applicants for social and rehabilitative services who responded to a request to participate in the research. For the most part, they were young, married, white females with some high school education. They represented average size families with minimal household incomes and described themselves as unemployed, either in the sense that they were housewives or out of work. Clients who were employed had been on their current jobs for only a short time.

Effectiveness Analysis   The central question for the effectiveness analysis was whether coordinated or coordinated/case-managed clients tended to report greater need satisfaction or personal growth than clients in the traditionally served group. Results revealed no significant differences in terms of need satisfaction. Hence, the coordinated and coordinated/case-managed approaches as implemented in the Project appeared to have no measurable impact on client need satisfaction or self-development.

The effectiveness analysis did, however, reveal some trends of interest, particularly on the Human Service Scale. Specifically, the coordinated/case-managed approach was related to moderate, yet nonsignificant, gains on the physiological, family, and social subscales, as well as in the total score. A similar trend appeared in the analysis of improvement from pretest to posttest on self-esteem. As with the Human Service Scale comparisons, the largest effect seemed to be with the coordinated/case-managed group followed by the coordinated and then the traditional group.

Efficiency Analysis   Although all groups were comparable in the number of potential referrals for client and client household, the coordinated/case-managed approach was associated with a higher percentage of clients following up on potential referrals, with a higher rate of total referrals, and with a lower incidence of duplicated referrals. Also, more new referrals actually got into service for the coordinated/case-managed group than for the other two groups.

Responsiveness Analysis   All groups were satisfied with services received, and there were no overall statistical differences in client satisfaction. Comparing client satisfaction across groups poses a logical problem, because clients did not know what else might have been possible for them and their households in the other experimental approaches. Hence, each client's basis for satisfaction rested on past and current experiences with services or expectations as to what services should provide, rather than on some comparison with services being provided concurrently to the other client groups.

Although contrary to what one might expect from the systems theory point of view and the literature on the effects of team approaches, the service coordination strategies implemented at the Arkansas Services Center had minimal effect on client need satisfaction, self-development, and satisfaction. However, efficiency gains were derived from the coordination/case management strategy. Strictly speaking, these findings provide little support for the extra emphasis, personnel, and finances to implement a service coordination approach. Yet, there were trends suggesting potential benefits of the coordinated/case-managed approach that appeared even in the face of numerous limitations in the implementation of the Project, such as lack of Project impetus, lack of agency cooperation, funding problems, low morale among staff members, and only minimal application of the coordination/case management treatment (Roessler and Mack, 1976). These limitations represented significant barriers to service coordination that merit further discussion.

BARRIERS TO THE COORDINATION OF HUMAN SERVICE

A variety of explanations can be offered for the minimal impact made by the Regional Integrated Services (RIS) Project. From the perspective of the research staff, it seemed that the actual treatments proposed, i.e., integration and case management, were applied in only limited ways. Restricted application of the treatment quite logically placed limitations on its ability to affect client growth. The following material discusses a number of barriers encountered in efforts to implement regional integrated services.

Barrier: Authority and Leadership

Probably the chief barrier to the implementation of the RIS Project was in the area of authority and leadership. Because Arkansas Social and Rehabilitative Service (SRS) was not in a position to mandate agency cooperation with the experimental Project, it had to elicit cooperation from agencies already feeling the effects of recession, such as limited resources and time to meet growing human needs. The Project became one additional interference experienced by the agencies, an interference that was coupled with no real authority to cause service providers to respond to it.

The cooperative stance of SRS seemed to have an effect on Project leadership as well. Project leadership reacted as if their only alternative was to diplomatically secure cooperation from agencies to meet RIS needs. At times, Project administrators no doubt felt that they had little backing from SRS or little actual authority themselves, and so they were reluctant to press agencies for cooperation in such things as completing the common intake form, attending training programs, etc.

Due to lack of authority or other reasons, it was apparent that Project administrators were reluctant to initiate activities. Lack of initiative from RIS became a standard operating mode for the first two years of the Project. Only minimal efforts were made to take the Project to agency personnel through training and information sessions. Hence, agency personnel reported that they were unaware of the goals, purposes, and achievements of the Project. One might hear agency personnel comment, "I don't see that they have done anything," and "The Project serves no useful purposes as far as we are concerned" (Roessler and Mack, 1975b).

The final problem noted in the leadership area had to do with excessive delegation. Perceiving his role as one of an expediter and delegator, the Project director delegated Project implementation of the previously designed system to the assistant director. The assistant director turned the design of the Project details over to the case managers. Although initially eager to become active in the new system, the case managers later resented the additional responsibility because they felt it not only detracted from their client service program, but it also placed inappropriate demands and stresses on their job role.

Barrier: Involvement

Related to the leadership issue, a problem also developed in the area of involvement. Project planning in its early phases seemed to occur without involvement of agency personnel at the Arkansas Services Center site. One division of SRS developed a functional and comprehensive set of flow charts diagramming the service integration system. Although the system itself seemed quite workable, it was developed without the assistance of service delivery personnel at Jonesboro. Instead, they were presented with a master plan for a project structure without having any part in its development. This imposition of what might be called an "outgroup product" contributed to the forms of agency resistance experienced during training sessions when Project staff felt obliged to defend the Project rather than to train personnel in the skills of completing the common intake form. The low rate of return of common intake forms might also be attributed to the lack of involvement that agency personnel felt they had in the development of Project directions.

Barrier: Definition of Terms

Another significant problem, heightened by the uncertainty always caused by change, was the ambiguity of the Project's intent. Both federal legislation and the Project proposal were unclear as to the meaning of several key terms relative to a service integration system.

For example, the difficulty of translating federal legislation into program activities noted by Weiss (1973) occurred for the RIS Project. According to Weiss (1973), legislation is often stated in inflationary promises or political language that is extremely vague due to its lack of operational specificity. The legislative base for the Regional Integrated Services Project was the Allied Services Act first proposed to Congress in 1972. The intent of the bill was to help clients achieve their maximum potential for eventual personal independence, dignity, and economic self-sufficiency through coordinated provision of services. The ambiguous terminology of the legislation first created a problem in determining what exactly was meant by coordination or integration. Arkansas SRS interpreted it to mean orchestration of service delivery through an organizational process that did not negate existing agency integrity, rather than any merging of agencies under the Department of Social and Rehabilitative Services.

Other definitional and, eventually, operational problems were encountered as the Project staff attempted to specify the generalities of the proposal. Issues had to be resolved as to who would do intake and whether that intake should be for the purposes of referral or indepth staffing. Differences regarding development of the common intake form and the case manager's role also served to further delay the implementation of the service integration program.

However, it seemed that one of the biggest definitional problems was the meaning of integration. Some agency personnel felt that the intent of service integration was to merge agencies and budgets into a single superagency. Having to lump their clients together in one large agency would dilute their efforts to serve special client groups—a development that many had worked years to accomplish. Presumably, integration was presented as coordination of services and not merging of agency functions. But, for some agency personnel, the issue may never have been clarified to their satisfaction; thus, they saw the program as a threat to their existence.

Barrier: Funding Ambiguity

Typical of short-term research projects, the projection of limited funding created a serious morale problem for staff. At one point, rumors were rampant that the Project would not be funded for a third year, which led personnel to feel extremely insecure and, in fact, to spend undue time either worrying about their job and/or actively seeking another one. It goes without saying that rumors of funding termination had a serious effect on the commitment of Project personnel, both to the Project's aims and leadership. In fact, in a historical sense, it seems that the three years of funded activity in the Jonesboro program actually purchased one year of active Project work. The first year was spent defining and developing Project objectives and operations, and the second year was spent in attempting to implement those objectives. In the third year, the staff was concerned with securing new positions after termination of funding of the Project.

Barrier: Situational Factors

Other problems or situational factors beyond the Project's control occurred concurrently. For example, changes in agency status, such as the shift of adult public assistance clients to Social Security from Social Services, had an effect on the Project. As a result of the client transfer, Social Services lost 25 positions, and, hence, was less able than ever to complete the common intake forms for the RIS Project. Some agencies, such as Public Health, which lacked staff to complete the intake procedures, were unable to participate unless Project personnel gathered the intake data.

Overview

Over all, a number of barriers limited the extent to which service integration could be implemented at the Arkansas Services Center. Barriers in authority, leadership, involvement, Project design, definition of terms, and concurrent agency changes in a time of recession affected the impact of both integration and case-managed experimental conditions. The very existence of these barriers raises an interesting question as to whether or not there really is a need for coordination projects. Possibly, interagency linkages are occurring, and these barriers were the result of feelings that the Project was either unnecessary or detrimental to service provision.

To the contrary, it seems that the barriers were symptomatic of needs that continue to exist in social and rehabilitative service delivery. A recent review (Regional Program Section, 1974) completed by SRS regional coordinators in 1974 underscores the need for efforts to coordinate social and rehabilitative services. From the point of view of SRS regional program personnel, the following problems still are characteristic of social and rehabilitative services:

1. There is inadequate understanding by divisions of each other's service roles, organizational channels, and proper staff contacts in regard to client services.
2. There is insufficient communication among division service delivery personnel working on or in close connection with individual case actions. Also, service supervisors do not have good cross-communications with each other.
3. Multi-divisional case planning is not being accomplished but should be. We need a systematic way of supporting case planning efforts in making sure those efforts will be extended.
4. There is a definite need for increased client advocacy internal to the SRS system; an advocacy channel from individual worker to the regional executive committee, as a formalized and sanctioned process, should be developed.
5. There is a need for all divisions' community-based workers and

supervisors to be trained in multi-agency work with multi-problem families.

6. A need exists to formalize referral procedures. Also, divisional communications with each other should be formalized regarding significant case actions, such as closure, inability to provide needed services, etc.

7. A need for far greater individual motivation on the part of caseworkers, supervisors, and administrators to engage in client problem-solving processes exists. Currently, the trend is to rely on cut-and-dried procedures with inadequate creativity if procedures do not take care of the problem.

8. Extensive training is needed in the area of learning to be helpful in conversations with clients. We are too often rude, inflexible, and impatient with clients (Regional Program Section, 1974).

Although the problems stimulating the development of the RIS Project continue to exist from the SRS point of view, it may be that agency personnel and administrators see no need for services coordination efforts. For this reason, they resist the idea of integration and block its implementation. However, data collected by the research staff in a survey of agency personnel at the Arkansas Services Center do not support the hypothesis that agency personnel reject the idea of services coordination (Roessler and Mack, 1975b).

Agency administrators and service providers at the Arkansas Services Center evaluated the concept of service integration positively, but they did not have such a positive perception of the RIS Project. Services Center personnel felt both uninformed about the Project's purposes, and that the Project expected them to commit excessive time to its needs. Regarding the Project itself, 63% reported either a neutral or a negative evaluation.

Yet, 87% of the Services Center personnel believed that services coordination could help clients. They remained open as to who should provide coordinated functions for a client household, e.g., an independent broker advocate, a primary agency representative, or a committee. However, these same service personnel were interested in seeing the processes of coordination underway.

Interestingly, over 60% of the agency personnel surveyed supported the basic structural components of regional integrated services. They felt that a coordination program must have a common intake form, a central referral mechanism, central records, co-location of agencies, and inclusion of other community agencies.

They reemphasized significant elements of the RIS program, such as common intake, case management, information sharing, and progress monitoring.

From the point of view of SRS personnel and individual agency service providers, the need exists for efforts to coordinate social and rehabilitative services. Having learned that the implementation of the Regional Integrated Services Project at the Arkansas Services Center had minimal impact, the question becomes one of "How could the Project have been improved?" The final section presents tentative recommendations for implementing services coordination projects. These recommendations, rather than being panaceas, represent experiences that may be useful to others involved in developing interagency coordination.

RECOMMENDATIONS FOR
IMPLEMENTATION OF SERVICE COORDINATION

A Common Goal

One recommendation for future service coordination efforts is that a common goal be identified. It is important that this goal evolve from individuals actually involved in the program's implementation and be accepted by others affected by the project. For example, a coordination project in Cleveland dealt with the common goal issue by identifying the meaning of agency coordination as "people renewal." Key activities of the Cleveland coordination project involved: 1) specifying the values to be gained by agency participation, 2) stipulating membership contingencies so that agencies could work together without fear of loss of autonomy, 3) providing communication links between agencies, 4) providing positive influence for interagency involvement, 5) providing for maintenance of the system and mechanisms to work through agency misunderstandings, 6) providing consultation toward helping agencies deal with one another, and 7) illustrating areas of common interest among agencies (O'Toole et al., 1972, pp. 7-8).

Involvement

Efforts to build understanding also require involvement of all participants in efforts to develop a program to meet common needs.

The program design itself should not be an outside master plan but rather be a product of those affected by the project.

Leadership

Obviously, the need to minimize service duplication and maximize service coordination to meet the needs of the entire client household is important to both those in service coordination projects and in individual agencies. To meet these needs, it may be necessary to have one division or agency within social and rehabilitative services take the leadership in services coordination. Such was done with the Cleveland project described by O'Toole et al. (1972). Collaborative agency efforts to develop coordinative structures drawing on the planning and financial resources of SRS could go a long way toward overcoming the problems of leadership, authority, and commitment previously mentioned.

Program Design

It is obvious that any project will be only as good as its original blueprint. For services coordination projects, it is necessary to define operationally the key terms such as coordination, case management, progress monitoring, common intake, etc. The first step is to emphasize coordination rather than integration, and define coordination as collaborative interagency linkages designed to assist the total client household. By making it very clear that the project is not attempting to merge budgets or agencies, but rather to develop coordinated services, agency autonomy would not be threatened.

Communication

The administration of any coordination project should keep agency personnel informed of project activities. Agency personnel will require training in areas having to do with common intake, case management, case monitoring, etc. Furthermore, agency personnel need to know the effect the project is having on key outcome areas, such as service effectiveness, efficiency, and responsiveness.

Community Relationships

Outside community agencies provide valuable resources for coordination projects. First, if trained in completing the common intake form, they can perform a valuable case finding function. Furthermore, services provided by these agencies are helpful to many families in need.

One Approach

Both SRS regional coordinators and agency personnel recognize a need for efforts to improve coordination of social and rehabilitative services. Though it is not fully agreed upon as to who should actually coordinate these services—an independent broker advocate, a committee, a lead agency representative—it is obvious that services coordination rests on accomplishing three important tasks for a client household: 1) needs analysis for all household members, 2) counseling, and 3) coordination. Needs analysis refers to a process for identifying the needs of client household members that can be met through social and rehabilitative services. The counseling function requires the ability to relate to people in a helpful way. Coordination of services emphasizes techniques for providing clients with an overview of an integrated service program for them and their households, and for monitoring case progress, entering new information into the system, and noting closure or continued service for the clients. The following list represents a step-by-step approach for implementing case management that has grown from the three year experience with regional integrated services at the Arkansas Services Center.

Steps in a Case Management
Approach to Services Coordination

1. When clients contact individual SRS agencies, they complete a common intake form that is routed to the case manager.
2. The case manager reviews the common intake form for every client and the client's household.
3. If the case manager has no need to meet with the client, the case manager makes appropriate referrals for the client's household.
4. The case manager sends a letter to the client listing referrals and means of contacting individual agencies.
5. If the case manager identifies additional needs on the common intake form, if he/she recognizes a situation that requires coordination of a case manager, or if he/she cannot clarify the need picture of the total client household, the case manager makes an appointment to see the client.
6. In cases where client and case manager must meet, the case manager begins by explaining his/her coordination role.
7. Using the common intake form, the case manager and client

discuss the client's and his/her household needs to determine completeness of the common intake form.

8. Needs of the client and his/her household members are identified, ranked, and translated into referrals.

9. Client and case manager discuss the referrals and what the client and his/her household members must do to receive agency services.

10. Barriers to receiving social and rehabilitative services are identified and ways to overcome them are discussed.

11. The case manager notifies agencies of the client's and his/her household's potential eligibilities. All relevant case data are then circulated to involved agencies.

12. The case manager checks on client contact with the agencies and follows up with the client regarding lack of contact.

13. As new information regarding the client household becomes available, the case manager routes it to appropriate agencies.

14. The case manager monitors case progress.

15. The case manager notes either closure of individual agencies or continued service where appropriate.

16. The case manager, at a later date, follows up with the client and his/her household to determine how well the original needs identified on the common intake form have been and are being met.

17. Additional services may be instituted as a result of the long term follow-up (Roessler and Mack, 1975a).

SUMMARY

Improving psychosocial adjustment to disability requires a multi-faceted service program in both field and facility settings. A field setting approach to service coordination that emphasizes meeting the multiple needs of clients and their households is discussed. Based on a systems theory perspective that is consistent with the interaction model of behavior, service coordination is accomplished through a team approach to case planning and service delivery. Research suggests that service coordination efforts must meet two needs in order to be effective. The first need pertains to client requirements: service coordination projects must provide systems for client participation in case planning and for counselor management of case progress. Second, administrative procedures must be specified and communicated to all service personnel. A service coordination system at the

Arkansas Services Center in Jonesboro endeavored to meet these client and administrative requirements. Although research results indicated that the Project had only a minimal effect on service effectiveness, noticeable gains were reported in terms of service efficiency. A number of barriers to greater Project effectiveness were noted, such as the lack of Project authority and leadership, the need for greater involvement of agency personnel, the lack of clarity regarding such terms as integration and coordination, the lack of security regarding funding, and unexpected situational factors, such as decreases in agency personnel. Recommendations for future implementation of service coordination projects stressed needs for a common goal, early involvement of all participants, strong agency leadership, an operational scheme for meeting client and administrative requirements, and utilization of community resources.

References

AAHPER. 1965. Youth Fitness Test Manual. Rev. Ed. American Association of Health, Physical Education, and Recreation, Washington, D.C.

Abramson, A. S. 1967. Modern concepts of management of the patient with spinal cord injury. Archives of Physical Medicine and Rehabilitation 48: 113–121.

Adams, H. 1972. Psychology of Adjustment. Ronald Press, New York.

Aiken, M., DiTomaso, N., Hage, H., and Zeitz, G. 1972. The coordination of services for the mentally retarded: A comparison of five community efforts. (Research Grant 15-P-552-13/5-03.) Rehabilitation Services Administration, Washington, D.C.

Albrecht, G. (ed.) 1976. The Sociology of Physical Disability and Rehabilitation. University of Pittsburgh Press, Pittsburgh.

Anthony, W., Margoles, A., and Collingwood, T. 1974. Rehabilitation counseling: A decisive approach. Journal of Rehabilitation 40(3):18–20.

Arkansas Rehabilitation Service. 1961. This is one way. (R&D Grant 147.) Office of Vocational Rehabilitation, Washington, D.C.

Armstrong, H., and Bakker, C. 1976. Behavioral self-analysis in the medical curriculum. Journal of Medical Education 51(9):758–762.

Ayer, M. J., Thoreson, R. W., and Butler, A. J. 1966. Predicting rehabilitation success with the MMPI and demographic data. Personnel and Guidance Journal 44:631–637.

Baker, M. J., and Sawyer, H. 1971. Adjustment Services in Rehabilitation: Emphasis on Human Change. Rehabilitation Services Education and Department of Vocational and Adult Education, Auburn University, Al.

Bakker, C. B. 1967. Psychological factors in angina pectoris. Psychosomatics 8:43–49.

Barker, R. G., Wright, B. A., Meyerson, L., and Gonick, M. R. 1953. Adjustment to Physical Handicap and Illness: A Survey of the Social Psychology of Physique and Disability. Rev. Ed. Social Science Research Council, New York.

Barry, J. R., Dunteman, G. E., and Webb, M. W. 1968. Personality and motivation in rehabilitation. Journal of Counseling Psychology 15:237–244.

Barry, J. R., and Malinovsky, M. R. 1965. Client Motivation for Rehabilitation: A Review. Regional Rehabilitation Research Institute, Gainesville, Fl.

Barton, K., and Cattell, R. B. 1972. Personality before and after a chronic illness. Journal of Clinical Psychology 28:464–467.

Bass, B., and Leavitt, H. 1963. Some experiments in planning and operating. Management Science 9:574–585.

Bidwell, G., Berner, B., and Meier, R. 1972. Chronic disability post-hospital survey: A focus on ancillary service needs. Rehabilitation Psychology 19(2):80–84.

Biostatistics Unit. 1972. Patient and Program Evaluation Recording. California Department of Mental Hygiene, Sacramento.

Bolton, B. 1972. Psychometric validation of a clinically derived typology of deaf rehabilitation clients. Journal of Clinical Psychology 28:22–25.

Bolton, B. 1974a. A factor analysis of personal adjustment and vocational measures of client change. Rehabilitation Counseling Bulletin 18:99–104.

Bolton, B. 1974b. Introduction to Rehabilitation Research. Charles C Thomas, Springfield, Ill.

Bolton, B. 1975. Factors contributing to successful rehabilitation of deaf clients. Journal of Rehabilitation of the Deaf 9(2):36–43.

Bolton, B. 1976. Rehabilitation programs. *In* B. Bolton (ed.), Psychology of Deafness for Rehabilitation Counselors, pp. 137–149. University Park Press, Baltimore.

Bolton, B. 1977a. Evidence for the 16PF primary and secondary factors. Multivariate Experimental Clinical Research 3(1):1–15.

Bolton, B. 1977b. Psychologist versus client perspectives in the assessment of psychopathology. Applied Psychological Measurement 1:533–542.

Bolton, B. 1978a. Review of the Sixteen Personality Factor Questionnaire. In The Eighth Mental Measurements Yearbook. Gryphon Press, Highland Park, N. J.

Bolton, B. 1978b. Client and counselor perspectives in the assessment of client adjustment. Rehabilitation Counseling Bulletin 21 (June). In press.

Bolton, B. 1978c. Dimensions of client change: A replication. Rehabilitation Counseling Bulletin 22 (September). In press.

Bolton, B., and Milligan, T. 1976. The effects of a systematic physical fitness program on clients in a comprehensive rehabilitation center. American Corrective Therapy Journal 30:41–46.

Bors, E. 1956. The challenge of quadriplegia. Bulletin of the Los Angeles Neurological Society 21:105–123.

Bradshaw, B., and Straker, M. 1974. A special unit to encourage giving up patienthood. Hospital and Community Psychiatry 25(3):164–165.

Brien, R. L., Kleiman, J., and Eisenman, R. 1972. Personality and drug use: Heroin, alcohol, methodrine, mixed drug dependency and the 16 P.F. Corrective Psychiatry and Journal of Social Therapy 18:22–23.

Burdsal, C., and Bolton, B. 1978. An item factoring of 16PF-E: Further evidence concerning Cattell's normal personality sphere. Journal of General Psychology. In press.

Buros, O. K. (ed.) 1975. Personality Tests and Reviews II. The Gryphon Press, Highland Park, N.J.

Cantril, H. 1965. The Pattern of Human Concerns. Rutgers University Press, New Brunswick, N.J.

Carkhuff, R. 1969. Helping and Human Relations. Holt, Rinehart, & Winston, New York.

Carkhuff, R. 1971. The Development of Human Resources. Holt, Rinehart, & Winston, New York.

Cattell, R. B. 1946. The Description and Measurement of Personality. World, New York.

Cattell, R. B. 1957. Personality and Motivation Structure and Measurement. World, New York.

Cattell, R. B. 1973. Personality and Mood by Questionnaire. Jossey-Bass, San Francisco.

Cattell, R. B., Eber, H. W., and Tatsuoka, M. M. 1970. Handbook for the Sixteen Personality Factor Questionnaire (16PF). Institute for Personality and Ability Testing, Champaign, Ill.

Cattell, R. B., Komlos, E., and Tatro, D. F. 1968. Significant differences of affective, paranoid, and non-paranoid schizophrenic psychotics on primary source traits in the 16 P.F. Multivariate Behavioral Research 3 (Special Issue):33–54.

Cautela, J. 1968. Behavior therapy and the need for behavioral assessment. Psychotherapy: Theory Research and Practice 5(3):175–179.

Christian, Q. A. 1969. Relationship between physical fitness and self concept. Unpublished doctoral dissertation, East Texas State University, Commerce.

Cobb, A. B. (ed.) 1973. Medical and Psychological Aspects of Disability. Charles C Thomas, Springfield, Ill.

Coch, L., and French, J. 1948. Overcoming resistance to change. In D. Cartwright and A. Zander (eds.), Group Dynamics: Research and Theory, pp. 336–350. Harper & Row, New York.

Collingwood, T. R. n.d. An orientation to therapeutic recreation: A training primer. Photocopy. Arkansas Rehabilitation Research and Training Center, Fayetteville.

Collingwood, T. R. 1972a. The effects of systematic physical, intellectual, and emotional personal adjustment programs. Research Report. Arkansas Rehabilitation Research and Training Center, Fayetteville.

Collingwood, T. R. 1972b. Physical fitness: A process goal for rehabilitating clients. Rehabilitation Research and Practice Review 3(3):71–75.

Collingwood, T. R., and Willett, L. 1971. The effects of physical training upon self-concept and body attitude. Journal of Clinical Psychology 27: 411–412.

Collins, H. A., Burger, G. K., and Doherty, D. D. 1970. Self-concept of EMR and nonretarded adolescents. American Journal of Mental Deficiency 75:285–289.

Colman, A. 1971. Social rejection, role conflict, and adjustment: psychological consequences of orthopaedic disability. Perceptual and Motor Skills 33:907–910.

Cook, D. 1976. Psychological aspects of spinal cord injury. Rehabilitation Counseling Bulletin 19:535–543.

Cook, D., and Roessler, R. 1977. Spinal cord injury in Arkansas: Rehabilitation service provision and client characteristics. Research Report. Arkansas Rehabilitation Research and Training Center, Fayetteville.

Cordaro, L., and Shontz, F. 1969. Psychological situations as determinants of self-evaluations. Journal of Counseling Psychology 16:575–578.

Davidoff, I., Lauga, A., and Walzer, R. 1969. The mental health rehabilitation worker: A new member of the psychiatric team. Community Mental Health Journal 5(1):46–54.

Dean, S. 1971. The role of self-conducted group therapy in psychorehabilitation: A look at Recovery, Inc. American Journal of Psychiatry 127(7):110–113.

De Cencio, D. V., Leshner, M., and Leshner, B. 1968. Personality characteristics of patients with chronic obstructive pulmonary emphysema. Archives of Physical Medicine and Rehabilitation 49:285–290.

DeMann, M. 1963. A predictive study of rehabilitation counseling outcomes. Journal of Counseling Psychology 10:340–343.

DePalma, N., and Clayton, H. D. 1958. Scores of alcoholics on the Sixteen Personality Factor Questionnaire. Journal of Clinical Psychology 14:390–392.

Dinardo, Q. 1971. Psychological adjustment to spinal cord injury. Unpublished doctoral dissertation, University of Houston, Texas.

Dinsdale, S. M., Lesser, A. L., and Judd, F. 1971. Critical psychosocial variables affecting outcome in a regional spinal cord center. Proceedings of the Veterans Administration Spinal Cord Injury Conference 18:193–196.

Dobson, M. 1969. Mental problems in rheumatoid arthritis. British Medical Journal 4:319.

Dobson, M., Tattersfield, A., Adler, M., and McNicol, M. 1971. Attitudes and long-term adjustment of patients surviving cardiac arrest. British Medical Journal 3:207–212.

Dunn, D. J. 1969. Adjustment to spinal cord injury in the rehabilitation hosptial setting. Unpublished doctoral dissertation, University of Maryland, College Park.

D'Zurilla, T., and Goldfried, M. 1971. Problem solving and behavior modification. Journal of Abnormal Psychology 78(1): 107–126.

English, R. W. 1971. Combatting stigma towards physically disabled persons. Rehabilitation Research and Practice Review 2:19–27.

Epstein, S. 1973. The self-concept revisited: Or a theory of a theory. American Psychologist 28:404–416.

Eysenck, H. J. 1972. Primaries or second-order factors: A critical consideration of Cattell's 16PF battery. British Journal of Social and Clinical Psychology 11:265–269.

Falek, A., and Britton, S. 1974. Phases in coping. Social Biology 21(1):1–7.

Fishman, S. 1949. Self-concept and adjustment to leg prosthesis. Unpublished doctoral dissertation, Columbia University, New York.

Fitts, W. H. 1972a. The Self Concept and Psychopathology. Monograph No. 4. Counselor Recordings and Tests, Nashville, Tenn.

Fitts, W. H. 1972b. The Self Concept and Behavior: Overview and Supplement. Monograph No. 7. Counselor Recordings and Tests, Nashville, Tenn.

Fogel, M., and Rosillo, R. 1969. Correlation of psychological variables and progress in physical rehabilitation. Diseases of the Nervous System 30: 593–601.

Fordyce, W. F. 1964. Personality characteristics in men with spinal cord injury as related to manner of onset of disability. Archives of Physical Medicine and Rehabilitation 45:321–325.

Fordyce, W. 1971. Behavioral methods in rehabilitation. In W. Neff (ed.), Rehabilitation Psychology, pp. 74–108. American Psychological Association, Washington, D.C.

Friermood, H. 1963. The YMCA Guide to Adult Fitness. Association Press, New York.

Gambrill, E., Thomas, E., and Carter, R. 1971. Procedure for sociobehavioral practice in open settings. Social Work 16(1):51–62.

Garrett, J., and Levine E. (eds.) 1962. Psychological Practices with the Physically Disabled. Columbia University Press, New York.

Gavales, D. 1966. Effects of combined counseling and vocational training on personal adjustment. Journal of Applied Psychology 50(1):18–21.

Gellman, W. 1959. Roots of prejudice against the handicapped. Journal of Rehabilitation 25:4–6.

Gilbert, D., and Lester, J. 1970. The relationship of certain personality and demographic variables to success in vocational rehabilitation. Research Report. Orthopedic Hospital, Los Angeles.

Gleser, G. C., and Gottschalk, L. A. 1967. Personality characteristics of chronic schizophrenics in relationship to sex and current functioning. Journal of Clinical Psychology 23:349–354.

Goldfried, M., and Merbaum, M. 1973. A perspective on self-control. In M. Goldfried and M. Merbaum (eds.), Behavior Change Through Self-Control, pp. 3–36. Holt, Rinehart, & Winston, New York.

Goldin, G. 1971. Rehabilitation and poverty. In W. Neff (Ed.), Rehabilitation Psychology, pp. 168–200. American Psychological Association, Washington, D.C.

Golightly, C., and Reinehr, R. C. 1969. 16PF profiles of hospitalized alcoholic patients: Replication and extension. Psychological Reports 24:543–545.

Goodkin, R. 1966. Case studies in behavioral research in rehabilitation. Perceptual and Motor Skills 23:171–182.

Goodyear, D., and Bitter, J. 1974. Goal attainment scaling as a program evaluation measure in rehabilitation. Journal of Applied Rehabilitation Counseling 5(1):19–26.

Gordon, E. 1971. Race, ethnicity, social disavantagement, and rehabilitation. In W. Neff (Ed.), Rehabilitation Psychology. pp. 201–214. American Psychological Association, Washington, D.C.

Gray, W., Duhl, F., and Rizzo, N. 1969. General Systems Theory and Psychiatry. Little-Brown, Boston.

Gressett, J. D. 1969. Prediction of job success following heart attack. Rehabilitation Counseling Bulletin 13:10–14.

Gross, W. F., and Alder, L. O. 1970. Aspects of alcoholics' self-concepts as measured by the Tennessee Self-Concept Scale. Psychological Reports 27: 431–434.

Gross, W. F., and Carpenter, L. C. 1971. Alcoholic personality: Reality or fiction? Psychological Reports 28:375–378.

Gruen, W. 1975. Effects of brief psychotherapy during the hospitalization period on the recovery process in heart attacks. Journal of Consulting and Clinical Psychology 43(2):223–232.

Guilford, J. P. 1959. Personality. McGraw-Hill Book Company, New York.

Hall, E. A. 1973. Self-concept development of active and recovered alcoholics. Unpublished doctoral dissertation, University of Arizona, Tucson.

Hansell, N. 1969. Patient predicament and clinical service: A system. In Gray, et al. (eds.), General Systems Theory and Psychiatry. Little-Brown, Boston.

Holland, C. 1970. An interview guide for behavioral counseling with parents. Behavior Therapy 1:70–79.

Houts, P., and Scott, R. 1972. Goal planning in mental health rehabilitation. (R&D Grant No. 15-P-55122/3-02). Rehabilitation Services Administration, Washington, D.C.

Hoy, R. M. 1969. The personality of inpatient alcoholics in relation to group psychotherapy, as measured by the 16PF. Journal of Studies on Alcohol 30:401–407.

Institute for Personality and Ability Testing. 1972. Manual for the 16PF. IPAT, Champaign, Ill.

Ivey, A., and Alschuler, A. 1973. An introduction to the field. Personnel and Guidance Journal 51(9):591–599.

Jensema, C. 1975. A statistical investigation of the 16PF form E as applied to hearing impaired college students. Journal of Rehabilitation of the Deaf 9(1):21–29.

Kahn, R., and Katz, D. 1953. Leadership practices in relation to productivity and morale. In D. Cartwright, and A. Zander (eds.), Group Dynamics, pp. 612–628. Harper & Row, New York.

Kanfer, F., and Saslow, G. 1965. Behavioral analysis: an alternative to diagnostic classification. Archives of General Psychiatry 12:529–538.

Kanfer, F. and Saslow, G. 1968. Behavioral diagnosis. In C. Franks (ed.), Assessment and Status of the Behavior Therapies and Associated Developments. McGraw-Hill Book Company, New York.

Katz, D., Macoby, N., and Morse, N. 1950. Productivity, Supervision, and Morale in an Office Situation. (Part I). Survey Research Center, Ann Arbor.

Kemp, B. J., and Wetmore, C. 1969-70. Adjustment factors among spinal cord injury patients: A follow-up study. Research Report. University of Southern California Rehabilitation Research and Training Center, Los Angeles.

Kemp, B. J., and Vash, C. L. 1971. Productivity after injury in a sample of spinal cord injured persons: A pilot study. Journal of Chronic Disorder 24:259–275.

Kidson, M. A. 1973. Personality and hypertension. Journal of Psychosomatic Research 17:35–41.

Kirchman, M. M. 1965. The personality of the rheumatoid arthritis patient. American Journal of Occupational Therapy 19:160–164.

Kirchner, J. H., and Marzolf, S. S. 1974. Personality of alcoholics as measured by Sixteen Personality Factor Questionnaire and House-Tree-Person color-choice characteristics. Psychological Reports 35:627–642.

Kiresuk, T., Salasin, S., and Garwick, G. 1972. The Program Evaluation Project: Overview. National Institute of Mental Health Program Evaluation Project (5RO1MH1678902). NIMH, Washington, D.C.

Kolb, D., and Boyatzis, R. 1970. Goal setting and self-directed behavior change. Human Relations 23:439–457.

Kolb, D., Winter, S., and Berlew, B. 1968. Self-directed change: two studies. Journal of Applied Behavioral Science 4(4):453–471.

Krumboltz, J. 1966. Behavioral goals for counseling. Journal of Counseling Psychology 13(2):153–159.

Krumboltz, J., and Thoresen, C. 1969. Behavioral Counseling: Cases and Techniques. Holt, Rinehart, and Winston, New York.

LaForge, R., and Suczek, R. 1955. Interpersonal dimension of personality: III. An interpersonal checklist. Journal of Personality 24:94–112.

Lake, D., Ritvo, M., and O'Brien, G. 1969. Applying behavioral science: Current projects. Journal of Applied Behavioral Sciences 5:367–390.

Lane, J. M., and Barry, J. R. 1970. Recent research on client motivation. Rehabilitation Research and Practice Review 1(4):5–25.

Langer, E., Janis, I., and Wolfer, J. 1975. Reduction of psychological stress in surgical patients. Journal of Experimental Social Psychology 11:155–165.

Lanyon, R. I. 1968. A Handbook of MMPI Group Profiles. University of Minnesota Press, Minneapolis.

Lasky, R., Dell Orto, A., and Marinelli, R. 1977. Structural experiential therapy applied to rehabilitation (SET-R). Paper presented at the American Personnel and Guidance Association Annual meeting, March, Dallas, Texas.

Lawlis, G. F., and Rubin, S. E. 1971. 16PF study of personality patterns in alcoholics. Quarterly Journal of Studies on Alcohol 32:318–327.

Lawrence, H., and Sundel, M. 1972. Behavior modification in adult groups. Social Work 17(2):34–43.

Lazarus, R. 1969. Patterns of Adjustment in Human Effectiveness. McGraw-Hill Book Company, New York.

Linkowski, D., and Dunn, M. 1974. Self-concept and acceptance of disability. Rehabilitation Counseling Bulletin 18(1):28–32.

Little, N. D., and Stewart, L. M. 1975. Vocational rehabilitation of spinal cord injured individuals. In M. J. Fuhrer (ed.), Selected Research Topics in Spinal Cord Injury Rehabilitation, pp. 119–140. Texas Institute for Rehabilitation and Research, Houston.

Lowin, A. 1968. Participative decision-making: A model, literature, critique, and prescriptions for research. Organizational Behavior and Human Performance 3:68–106.

MacGuffie, R. 1970. Relationship between the social vocabulary index and the interaction scale and rehabilitation success. Journal of Counseling Psychology 17(3):289–290.

MacGuffie, R. A., Jansen, F. V., Samuelson, C. O., and McPhee, W. M. 1969. Self-concept and ideal-self in assessing the rehabilitation applicant. Journal of Counseling Psychology 16:157–161.

Mahoney, M., and Thoresen, C. 1974. Self-Control: Power to the Person. Brooks/Cole, Monterey, Ca.

Margolin, R. 1955. Member-employee program: New hope for the mentally ill. American Archives of Rehabilitation Therapy 3:69–81.

Marinelli, R. 1974. State anxiety in interactions with visibly disabled persons. Rehabilitation Counseling Bulletin 18(2):72–77.

Marinelli, R., and Dell Orto, A. (eds.) 1977. Psychological and Social Impact of Physical Disability. Springer, New York.

Mathias, R. E. S. 1955. An experimental investigation of the personality structure of chronic alcoholic, alcoholics anonymous, neurotic and normal groups. Unpublished doctoral dissertation, University of Buffalo, New York.

McDaniel, J. 1976. Physical Disability and Human Behavior. 2d Ed. Pergamon Press, New York.

McNickle, R. 1975. Report of the Comprehensive Service Needs Study. The Urban Institute, Washington, D.C.

McPhee, W. M., and Magleby, F. 1960. Success and failure in vocational rehabilitation. Personnel and Guidance Journal 38:497–499.

Means, B., and Roessler, R. 1976. Personal Achievement Skills Leader's Manual and Participant's Workbook. Arkansas Rehabilitation Research and Training Center, Fayetteville.

Meighan, T. 1970. An investigation of the self concept of blind and partially seeing adolescents and of the relation of their self concepts to academic achievement in language and paragraph reading. Unpublished doctoral dissertation, Catholic University, Washington, D.C.

Meissner, A. 1966. Adolescent attitudes toward self and toward disabled people. Unpublished doctoral dissertation, University of Wisconsin, Madison.

Miles, H., Waldfogel, S., Barrabee, E., and Cobb, S. 1954. Psychosomatic study of 47 young men with coronary artery disease. Psychosomatic Medicine 16:455–477.

Miller, D., Kunce, J., and Getsinger, S. 1972. Prediction of job success for clients with hearing loss. Rehabilitation Counseling Bulletin 16:21–28.

Milligan, T. 1976a. Physical Fitness Training for Rehabilitation Clients: An Instructor-Assisted Program Package: Instructor's Manual. Arkansas Rehabilitation Research and Training Center, Fayetteville.

Milligan, T. 1976b. Physical Fitness Training for Rehabilitation Clients: An Instructor-Assisted Program Package: Participant's Manual. Arkansas Rehabilitation Research and Training Center, Fayetteville.

Milligan, T. 1976c. Physical Fitness Training for Rehabilitation Clients: An Instructor-Assisted Program Package: Typescript of Daily Lectures. Arkansas Rehabilitation Research and Training Center, Fayetteville.

Milligan, T., and Roessler, R. 1977. Development and evaluation of a self-instructional physical fitness training program for spinal cord injured rehabilitation clients. Annual Report No. 13 (Project No. R-145). Arkansas Rehabilitation Research and Training Center, Fayetteville.

Mischel, W. 1968. Personality and Assessment. John Wiley, New York.

Mischel, W. 1973. Toward a cognitive social learning reconceptualization of personality. Psychological Review 80(4):252–283.

Mooney, R., and Gordon, L. 1950. Mooney Problem Checklists. Psychological Corporation, New York.

Mueller, A. 1962. Psychological factors in rehabilitation of paraplegic patients. Archives of Physical Medicine and Rehabilitation 43:151–159.

Muhlern, T. J. 1975. Use of the 16PF with mentally retarded adults. Measurement and Evaluation in Guidance 8:26–28.

Neff, W., Novick, B., and Stern, B. 1968. A Follow-Up Counseling Program. Jewish Occupational Council, New York.

Nerviano, V., and Gross, W. 1973. A multivariate delineation of two alcoholic profile types on the 16PF. Journal of Clinical Psychology 29:371–374.

Newman, L. 1970. Instant placement: A new model for providing rehabilitation services within a community mental health program. Community Mental Health Journal 6(5):401–409.

O'Connor, J., and Leitner, L. 1971. Traumatic quadriplegia: A comprehensive review. Journal of Rehabilitation 37:14–20.

O'Toole, R., O'Toole, A., McMillan, R., and Lefton, M. 1972. The Cleveland rehabilitation complex. (Final Report SRS Grant RO-2594-G.) Vocational Guidance and Rehabilitation Services, Cleveland.

Phillip, A., and Cay, E. 1972. Psychiatric symptoms and personality traits in patients suffering from gastrointestinal illness. Journal of Psychosomatic Research 16:47–51.

Poor, C. 1975. Vocational rehabilitation of persons with spinal cord injuries. Rehabilitation Counseling Bulletin 18:264–271.

Pringle, M. 1964. The emotional and social readjustment of physically handicapped children: A review of the literature between 1928 and 1962. Educational Research 6:207–215.

Rabinowitz, H. 1961. Motivation for recovery: Four social-psychologic aspects. Archives of Physical Medicine and Rehabilitation 42:799–807.

Raths, L., Harmin, M., and Simon, S. 1966. Values and Teaching. Charles Merrill, Columbus, Oh.

Reagles, K., Wright, G., and Butler, A. 1970. Correlates of client satisfaction in an expanded vocational rehabilitation program. (Monograph 12, Series 2). Regional Rehabilitation Research Institute, Madison, Wi.

Regional Program Section. 1974. Department of Social and Rehabilitative Services, Little Rock, Ark.

Rehabilitation Services Administration. 1976. Research and Evaluation Strategy. Rehabilitation Services Administration, Office of Human Development, DHEW, Washington, D.C.

Roessler, R. 1972. Human dignity: an attainable goal. Rehabilitation Research and Practice Review 4(3):1–10.

Roessler, R. 1978. Personal Achievement Skills training with the visually handicapped. Rehabilitation Counseling Bulletin 21(June). In press.

Roessler, R., Bolton, B., Means, B., and Milligan, T. 1975. The effects of physical, intellectual, and emotional training on rehabilitation clients. The Journal of Applied Rehabilitation Counseling 6(2):106–112.

Roessler, R., Cook, D., and Lillard, D. 1976. The effects of systematic group counseling in work adjustment training. Research Report. Arkansas Rehabilitation Research and Training Center, Fayetteville.

Roessler, R., Cook, D., and Lillard, D. 1977. Effects of systematic group counseling on work adjustment clients. Journal of Counseling Psychology 24(4):313–317.

Roessler, R., and DeWeese, M. 1975. Personal Achievement Skills training in a classroom setting. Unpublished paper. Arkansas Rehabilitation Research and Training Center, Fayetteville.

Roessler, R., and Green, P. 1974. An evaluation of Personal Achievement Skills by rehabilitation personnel. Research Report. Arkansas Rehabilitation Research and Training Center, Fayetteville.

Roessler, R., and Mack, G. 1975a. Services integration final report. Research Monograph. Arkansas Rehabilitation Research and Training Center, Fayetteville.

Roessler, R., and Mack, G. 1975b. Jonesboro Service Coordination Project Quarterly Report (March). Arkansas Rehabilitation Research and Training Center, Fayetteville.

Roessler, R., and Mack, G. 1976. Evaluation of an experimental service coordination project. Journal of Applied Rehabilitation Counseling 7(3):149–157.

Roessler, R., Mack, G., and Statler, J. 1975. Experimental Case Management: Pilot Manual for Training Case Managers in Services Coordination Projects. Arkansas Rehabilitation Research and Training Center, Fayetteville.

Roessler, R., and Means, B. 1976a. Personal Achievement Skills Instructor's Supplement: Program Development and Evaluation Guidelines. Arkansas Rehabilitation Research and Training Center, Fayetteville.

Roessler, R., and Means, B. 1976b. Personnal Achievement Skills: An Introduction. Discussion Paper. Arkansas Rehabilitation Research and Training Center, Fayetteville.

Roessler, R., and Means, B. 1977. Personal Achievement Skills for the Visually Handicapped. Arkansas Rehabilitation Research and Training Center, Fayetteville.

Roessler, R., Means, B., and Cook, D. 1977. A structured group counseling format for rehabilitation settings. Rehabilitation Literature 38:193–195.

Roessler, R., Means, B., and Farley, R. 1977. Behavior Analysis Training: Counselor's Manual. Arkansas Rehabilitation Research and Training Center, Fayetteville.

Roessler, R., Milligan, T., and Ohlson, A. 1976. Personal adjustment training for the spinal cord injured. Rehabilitation Counseling Bulletin 19(4): 544–551.

Rosenthal, S., Aitken, R., and Zeally, A. 1973. The Cattell 16PF personality profile of asthmatics. Journal of Psychosomatic Research 17:9–14.

Rothfarb, H. 1970. A study of the psychological needs and self-esteem of college men who exercise regularly. Unpublished doctoral dissertation, Boston College, Mass.

Rotter, J. 1966. Generalized expectancies for internal versus external control of reinforcement. Psychological Monographs 80 (1, whole number 309).

Rubin, S., and Salley, K. 1973. Studies of prediction of rehabilitation client outcome. Research Report. Arkansas Rehabilitation Research and Training Center, Fayetteville.

Rucker, W., Arnspiger, D., and Brodbeck, A. 1969. Human Values and Education. Kendall-Hunt, Dubuque, Ia.

Safilios-Rothschild, C. 1970. The Sociology and Social Psychology of Disability and Rehabilitation. Random House, New York.

Schroedel, J. G., and Schiff, W. 1972. Attitudes towards deafness among several deaf and hearing populations. Rehabilitation Psychology 19:59–70.

Schurr, K., Joiner, L., and Towne, R. 1970. Self-concept research on the mentally retarded: A review of empirical studies. Mental Retardation 8: 39–43.

Schwartz, A., and Goldiamond, I. 1975. Social Casework: A Behavioral Approach. Columbia University Press, New York.

Schwartz, M., Dennerll, R., and Lin, Yi Guang. 1968. Neuropsychological and psychosocial predictors of employability in epilepsy. Journal of Clinical Psychology 24:174–177.

Sechrest, L., and Wallace, J. 1967. Psychology and Human Problems. Charles Merrill, Columbus, O.

Serban, G., and Katz, G. 1975. Schizophrenic performance on form E of Cattell's 16PF test. Journal of Personality Assessment 39:169–177.

Shekelle, R., and Ostfeld, A. 1965. Psychometric evaluations in cardiovascular epidemiology. Annals of the New York Academy of Sciences 126:696–705.

Shelsky, I. 1957. The effect of disability on self-concept. Unpublished doctoral dissertation, Columbia University, New York.

Shontz, F. 1970. Physical disability and personality: Theory and recent research. Psychological Aspects of Disability 17:51–69.

Shontz, F. 1971. Physical disability and personality. In W. Neff (ed.), Rehabilitation Psychology. American Psychological Association, Washington, D.C.

Shontz, F. 1975. The Psychological Aspects of Physical Illness and Disability. MacMillan, New York.

Siller, J. 1969. Psychological situation of the disabled with spinal cord injury. Rehabilitation Literature 30:290–296.

Siller, J. 1976. Attitudes toward disability. In H. Rusalem and D. Malikin (eds.), Contemporary Vocational Rehabilitation. New York University Press, New York.

Simon, J. 1971. Emotional aspects of physical disability. American Journal of Occupational Therapy 25:408–410.

Simon, S., Howe, L., and Kirschenbaum, H. 1972. Values Clarification: A Handbook of Practical Strategies for Teachers and Students. Hart, New York.

Sivadon, P., and Veil, C. 1968. Psychopathological incidence of occupational accident. Revue Internationale De Psychologie Applique 17(1):31–32.

Skinner, B. 1953. Science and Human Behavior. Macmillan, New York.

Skinner, B. 1966. What is the experimental analysis of behavior? Journal of the Experimental Analysis of Behavior 9(3):213–218.

Smith-Hanen, S. 1976. Socialization of the physically handicapped. Journal of Applied Rehabilitation Counseling 7(3):131–141.

Smits, S. 1964. Reactions of self and others to the obviousness and severity of physical disability. Unpublished doctoral dissertation, University of Missouri, Columbia.

Solomon, L., Berzon, B., and Davis, D. 1970. A personal growth program for self-directed groups. Journal of Applied Behavioral Science 6(4):427–451.

Spangler, D. 1966. Service Needs of Paraplegics and Quadriplegics. National Paraplegic Foundation, Chicago.

Spencer, L., Jr. 1973. Planning and organizing human services delivery systems. In Proceedings of a Seminar on Human Services Integration, pp. 8–26. (SRS Grant No. 09-56029/8-03). University of Denver, Denver, Co.

Spiegel, J. 1969. Environmental corrections as a systems process. In Gray, et al. (eds.), General Systems Theory and Psychiatry. Little-Brown, Boston.

Stewart, H. 1965. The relationship of physical illness to the IPAT 16 Personality Factors test. Journal of Clinical Psychology 21:264–266.

Stotsky, B., Mason, A., and Semaras, M. 1958. Significant figures in the rehabilitation of chronic mental patients. Journal of Chronic Diseases 7: 131–139.

Stubbins, J. (ed.) 1977. Social and Psychological Aspects of Disability. University Park Press, Baltimore.

Suchman, E. 1965. A model for research and evaluation of rehabilitation. In M. Sussman (ed.), Sociology and Rehabilitation. American Sociological Association, Washington, D.C.

Sussman, M. (ed.) 1965. Sociology and Rehabilitation. American Sociological Association, Washington, D.C.

Thomas, E., and Walter, C. 1973. Guidelines for behavioral practice in the open community agency: Procedure and evaluation. Behavioral Research and Therapy 11:193–205.

Thoreson, R., Smits, S., Butler, A., and Wright, G. 1968. Counselor Problems Associated with Client Characteristics. Wisconsin Studies in Vocational Rehabilitation, Monograph No. 3. Regional Rehabilitation Research Institute, Madison, Wi.

Trieschmann, R. 1974. Coping with the disability: A sliding scale of goals. Archives of Physical Medicine and Rehabilitation 55:556–560.

Trombly, C. 1966. Principles of operant conditioning: Related to orthotic training of quadriplegic patients. American Journal of Occupational Therapy 20(5):217–220.

Trotter, A., and Inman, D. 1968. The use of positive reinforcement in physical therapy. Physical Therapy 48(4):347–352.

Trybus, R. 1973. Personality assessment of entering hearing-impaired college students using the 16PF, form E. Journal of Rehabilitation of the Deaf 6(3):34–40.

Tucker, W. 1968. An investigation of the feasibility of using the 16PF questionnaire to identify the personality traits of physically handicapped college students. Unpublished doctoral dissertation, University of South Dakota, Vermillion.

Vernier, C., Stafford, J., and Krugman, A. 1958. A factor analysis of indices from four projective techniques associated with four different types of physical pathology. Journal of Consulting Psychology 22:433–437.

Wahler, H., Delbridge, C., and Clubb, C. 1969. Needed: competence rehabilitation. Proceedings of the ninth annual research meeting. Department of Institutions, State of Washington and the University of Washington, Research Report 2(2):April.

Walker, L., Adamson, F., Alexander, D., and Stoffelmayer, B. 1973. A negative correlation between improved production in psychiatric rehabilitation and social behaviour outside. British Journal of Psychiatry 123:409–412.

Warren, L., and Weiss, D. 1969. Relationship between disability type and measured personality characteristics. Proceedings of the 77th Annual Convention of the American Psychological Association 4:773–774.

Watson, D., and Tharp, R. 1972. Self-Directed Behavior: Self Modification for Personal Adjustment. Brooks/Cole, Monterey, Ca.

Waxman, W. 1960. Physical fitness developments for adults in the YMCA. In S. Staley (ed.), Exercise and Fitness. Athletic Institute Press, Champaign, Ill.

Weinberg-Asher, N. 1976. The effect of physical disability on self-perception. Rehabilitation Counseling Bulletin 20:15–20.

Weiner, H. 1964. Characteristics associated with rehabilitation success. Personnel and Guidance Journal 42:687–694.

Weiss, C. 1973. Between the cup and the lip. Evaluation 1(2):49–55.

Wickert, F. 1951. Turnover and employees' feelings of ego-involvement. Personnel Psychology 4:185–197.

Wiener, C. 1975. The burden of rheumatoid arthritis: Tolerating the uncertainty. Social Science and Medicine 9:97–104.

Wiener, D. 1948. Personality characteristics of selected disability groups. Journal of Clinical Psychology 4:285–290.

Williams, J. 1971. Manifest anxiety and self-concept: A comparison of blind and sighted adolescents. Unpublished doctoral dissertation, University of Maryland, College Park.

Wilson, T. 1969. Patterns of management and adaptations to organizational roles: A study of prison inmates. American Journal of Sociology pp. 146–164.

Winter, S., Griffith, J., and Kolb, D. 1968. Capacity for self-direction. Journal of Consulting and Clinical Psychology 32:35–41.

Wright, B. 1960. Physical Disability—A Psychological Approach. Harper & Row, New York.

Wright, B. A. 1975. Social-psychological leads to enhance rehabilitation effectiveness. Rehabilitation Counseling Bulletin 18(4):214–223.

Wright, G., Reagles, K., and Butler, A. 1969. The Wood County Project. (Final Report, RD Grant 1629). Regional Rehabilitation Research Institute Madison, Wi.

Wright, G., and Trotter, A. 1968. Rehabilitation Research. University of Wisconsin, Madison.

Zisfein, L., and Rosen, M. 1973. Personal adjustment training: A group counseling program for institutionalized mentally retarded persons. Mental Retardation 11:16–20.

Zisfein, L., and Rosen, M. 1974. Effects of a personal adjustment training group counseling program. Mental Retardation 12:50–53.

Author Index

Subject Index

Acceptance of disability, 16, 47–48
Achievement
  viewpoints of adjustment, 3–4
Adjustment
  achievement versus process in, 3–4
  behavioral orientation to, 42–43,
    128–129
  concepts of, 5–8, 18–19
  definition of, 3
  frames of reference on, 4–5
  and interaction position, 51–52
  measurement of, 5
  models of, 5–8, 18–19, 42
  process of, 1, 76
  psychosocial, 1–3, 5, 7–10
  relationship between psychosocial
    and vocational, 8–10
  services, 41–42, 145
  theory for services, 43–45, 49–50
  to reduced activity levels, 18
  training, 1–3, 7–8, 12, 41–43,
    52–55, 75–79, 82
Alcoholism, 25–26, 33–35
Amputation, 24
Arthritis, rheumatoid, and personality, 30–31
"As if" behavior, 15–16
Asthmatic patients and personality
  factor, 31
Attitudes
  prejudicial, sources of, 11–12
  toward disability, 1, 10–13, 54–55

Behavioral Analysis Training, 128–133
  and behavioral change strategies,
    129, 132
  enhancing personal adjustment
    with, 128
  goals and strategies in, 129–133,
    138–141
  phases of, 132–143
  readiness for, 130, 135–136
  self control and, 130–131, 137–138
  and stimulus control, 134–135

Behavioral coping model of adjustment, 18–19, 43–45
  and cultural relativity, 42–43
Blindness, 24
  and use of Personal Achievement
    Skills, 107–109
Body image, 13

Cognitive social learning theory
    approach to adjustment
  applications for adjustment
    services, 43–45
  as approach to assessing behavior,
    44
  and factors contributing to
    behavior change, 44–45
  view of individual differences,
    44–45
Compensation as a sign of failure to
    cope, 15
Containing effects of disability, 16, 18
Coordination of human services, 145,
    157–158
  approaches to, 150
  barriers to, 152–156
  and case management, 149–152,
    160–161
  client outcome and, 145–146
  effectiveness of, 148–152, 157–158
  implementation, 158–161
  and integration of services, 145–146,
    154, 157
  and mediated sharing approach,
    146
  and systems theory of service
    delivery, 147–148, 152
  vocational success and, 147
Coping
  behavioral model, 18–19, 41–42
  positive signs of, 16–18

Deafness, 34–35, 51, 53–54
Denial, 14, 17

181

DATE DUE